Knowledge Activism Beyond Theory

Knowledge Activism
Beyond Theory

A WORLDWIDE CALL TO ACTION

© 2016 R.S.Wafula and Joseph F. Duggan

Published by Borderless Press
Alameda, California
www.borderlesspress.com
info@borderlesspress.com

Design by Melody Stanford

All rights reserved. No part of this book may be reproduced or transmitted in any form or by any means, electronic or mechanical, including photocopy, recording, or any information storage and retrieval system, without prior permission from the publisher, except by a retriever who may quote brief passages in articles or reviews.

Although every precaution has been taken to verify the accuracy of the information contained herein, the author and publisher assume no responsibility for any errors or omissions. No liability is assumed for damages that may result from the use of information contained within.

Library of Congress Control Number: 2016958253

ISBN-13: 978-0-9962017-5-9
ISBN-10: 0-9962017-5-0

First edition

Printed in the United States of America

*We dedicate this book to
Majority World scholars whose voices
have been silenced, and to the
relentless efforts of knowledge activists
to reclaim those voices.*

CONTENTS

ACKNOWLEDGEMENTS _____ xi
LIST OF ABBREVIATIONS _____ xiii
INTRODUCTION
    R.S. WAFULA & JOSEPH F. DUGGAN _____ xv

I. *Knowledge Activism* JOSEPH F. DUGGAN

   A. Why this Book Matters _____ 1
   B. An Abbreviated Colonial Knowledge Simulation _____ 9
   C. Other Researchers in North America and Europe ____ 15

II. Epistemological Principles for *Knowledge Activism* R.S. WAFULA

   A. Mapping Colonial Knowledge Systems _____ 17
   B. Contesting Colonial Knowledge Systems _____ 26
   C. From Theory to Praxes: Levinas' Hermeneutics of "The Face" and Ricoeur's philosophy of "Oneself as Another" _____ 44

III. Recasting Subalternity, Marginality and Privilege as Fluid Identities R.S. WAFULA

   A. Fluid Subalternity, Marginality, and Privilege Between Euro-American Contexts and Majority World Contexts ___ 51

    B. Fluid Subalternity, Marginality, and Privilege Between Diaspora Majority World Scholars and 'On-the-Continent' Majority World Scholars _____ 63

    C. Fluid Subalternity, Marginality, and Privilege Among Majority World Scholars in the Majority World Geopolitical Settings_____ 73

IV. Crossroads: When Majority and Minority World Scholars Meet R.S. WAFULA & JOSEPH F. DUGGAN

    A. Majority World Scholar: Intersections Between Empathy and *Knowledge Activism* — Wafula _____ 79

    B. Minority World Scholarship — Duggan _____ 86

        An Unfolding Autobiographical Path to Knowledge Activism _____ 87

        The Struggle and Gift to Speak _____ 89

        Initial Recognition of the Knowledge System and Its Privileges _____ 92

        "I found space for my voice here." _____ 93

        Global Network and Knowledge Sharing _____ 95

    Knowledge Activism Within the Existing Knowledge System: Palgrave _____ 97

    Knowledge Activism Within the Existing Knowledge System: Journals _____ 98

    Knowledge Activism — The Break Away from Institutions: Borderless Press _____ 99

V. *Knowledge Activism* After Theory
R.S. WAFULA & JOSEPH F. DUGGAN

    A. The Way *Knowledge Activism* Theory Becomes Praxis — Duggan _____ 105

        When Scholars Look the Other Way _____ 106

        When Faculty Teach Privileg _____ 108

        Reactive Responses to Invisible Publishers _____ 109

      Impermeable Resistance to Change _____ 111

      Economic Realities Behind the Scenes _____ 112

      Majority World Authors Left Without Good Choices ___ 114

  B. *Knowledge Activism* Cartography: Workshop, Pre-peer Review, Scholar Mentor, Writing Residency, Peer Review, Publishing, Alternate Reading Lenses, Economics — Wafula _____ 116

      Major Euro-American Publishers: A Bitter Personal Encounter _____ 116

      Borderless Press: A Different Kind of Press _____ 118

  C. *Knowledge Activism*: Knowledge for Social Change — Wafula _____ 126

      Research Question as a Reflection of Sociopolitical and Economic Mirror of the Researcher _____ 126

VI. Changes That Liberate Colonial Knowledge
JOSEPH F. DUGGAN

Slow Change _____ 130

Disruptive Publishing _____ 131

Conclusions — Wafula and Duggan _____ 135

Appendix — *Knowledge Activism*: Self-Assessment and Development

BIBLIOGRAPHY _____ 147

ACKNOWLEDGEMENTS

Getting involved in organizing and executing two Writing and Publishing workshops at St. Paul's University in Limuru Kenya in 2015 and 2016 has been an eye-opening experience for us. We came face to face with the material contingencies of knowledge marginalization as we encountered over one hundred scholars whose works have faced enormous challenges in terms of seeking publication. We would like to thank these scholars for the stories they shared with us and for undertaking a journey with us to work towards scholarly justice. Their stories are a part of the reason that we write this book.

We offer our special thanks to our production editor Melody Stanford for the design of the book's cover and layout of the book. We acknowledge our copy editor Caroline Brennan who meticulously read the manuscript and corrected many of our human errors. This work is so much better because of her commitment.

We would like to thank our families who have as much dedication and passion as we do in calling the world to attention about knowledge marginalization. They have encouraged us, support us, and given us the reason to write this work. We want to be particularly grateful to Stefani

(Duggan's wife) who became ill while we were writing this book. Stefani was passionately committed to the book's multi-year development even contributing the language of *knowledge activist* "mindset" prior to her illness and then during the course of her illness has generously offered Joe space to write. We want to thank Jane (Wafula's wife) who allowed Wafula time to travel to St. Paul's in Kenya for the workshops. She has also taken the larger share of the parental caring of three lovely energetic children (Wekesa, Simiyu, and Nasimiyu). We also want to thank Wafula's children who allowed their father time to write. Without our families' support in its many forms it would have been impossible to complete this book in a timely manner.

LIST OF ABBREVIATIONS

OTSSA — The Old Testament Society of Southern Africa

JSLAS — Journal of the Society for Latin American Studies

JH & SS — Journal of Humanities & Social Sciences

JPPLHW — Journal of Peripheral Cultural Production of the Luso-Hispanic World

INTRODUCTION

R.S. Wafula & Joseph F. Duggan

Through this book we invite you to join Postcolonial Networks and Borderless Press in a worldwide *knowledge activism* movement. Your participation in *knowledge activism* is vital for collective impact and transformation of knowledge as we each deploy anti-colonial knowledge practices. Every one of us must take responsibility for taking on an anti-colonial *knowledge activist* mindset. In the Appendix readers will find a *Knowledge Activism* Self-Assessment and Development tool to assist you in making choices in every stage of knowledge development no matter your role: student, researcher, faculty, librarian, copy editor and publisher. We all have a critical role to play and will only be successful when we work together. In this book we have outlined our *knowledge activism*.

Knowledge activism precedes our naming of the movement in this book. In this manner we believe our book on *knowledge activism* is best situated among the interests of a diverse group of independent presses that recognize and serve excluded communities whose voices have been inaudible to most readers. These are publishers who stand in solidarity with authors, often people of color, women and other minorities who have been systematically ignored and whose works are not deemed of value fit for publication.

Karl Marx did not use the words *knowledge activism* when he sought a publisher for *The Communist Manifesto*, but in his distrust of mainstream publishers he practiced a knowledge activism mindset and acted as a *knowledge activist*.

Aunt Lute did not use the words *knowledge activism* to describe their establishment of a press in 1982 to publish feminist women of color, but in their recognition of lack of access for authors like Gloria Anzaldua and Audre Lorde they practiced a *knowledge activism* mindset and have acted as *knowledge activists*.

Universities in Africa do not use the words *knowledge activism* to describe their decolonial questions about the role of the university, knowledge production and development, but in their reconstructive efforts they practice a *knowledge activism* mindset and act as *knowledge activists*.

Indigenous women authors in India practice a *knowledge activism* mindset when, tired of waiting to be published by North American and European publishers, they claim their authority as *knowledge activists* and self-publish a book for local use with the possibility to be read by readers beyond their nation.

While all these are the works of *knowledge activism*, the lack of a documented *knowledge activist* mindset and stories of *knowledge activists* further delays others from hearing the voices of authors in excluded communities. In this book we seek to migrate from the sole narration of decolonial methodologies into *knowledge activist* mindsets where theory and praxis meet to challenge privileged knowledge creation, publishing and reading practices. We offer our vision through a *knowledge activism* mindset and suggest ways that our readers are able to accept their ethical responsibility as *knowledge activists*.

The entire knowledge production system requires a *knowledge activism* mindset shift before the dominant colonial *knowledge system* is replaced. The *knowledge activist mindset* cannot be the choice of a few *knowledge activists*. The *knowledge activist* mindset must become the practice of every author, professor, copy editor, peer reviewer, publisher, librarian and reader as well as every other actor in the knowledge economy that has a role in bringing a book from an author to their readers.

More decolonial theories and greater knowledge will not compel the colonial knowledge economy and its actors to urgently advocate a *knowledge activist* mindset. The primary actors of the knowledge economy are too frantically busy reaping the final benefits of a dying ecosystem as they receive the coveted call of a prestigious editor, are invited to double peer review for a prestigious journal that looks good on their CV, naively accept the last tenure appointments, miserly bank small royalties that make their efforts seem of some value and nonchalantly accept that their book will only be read in research libraries and that general interest readers have no access to their knowledge. The primary actors in the knowledge economy have little awareness or interest that the ecosystem is polluted and that some authors especially in the Majority World[1] are

---

1. Throughout this book we will use the term Majority World to refer to marginalized parts of the world; namely Africa, Latin America and Asia. In contrast we use the term Minority World to refer to the parts of the world that can be defined as centers of privilege; namely Europe and North America. We use these terms "subversively" and in protest in line with scholarship that contests the idea that the Majority World, which represents the largest human habitation, has been defined and controlled by the Minority World, which represents itself as the center of humanity, even as it posits the least populated human inhabitants. See Emmanuel Narokobi, A. N., "'Majority World' — A New Word

gasping for air, thirsty, hungry to be heard and to have impact through their research and writing.

Note the pattern in the above offered examples. The major publishers have been easily scapegoated, enabling others to avoid their individual ethical responsibilities. Recognition of voice and invitation to the table is always about power, who has power and who does not. The rise of some independent presses like Aunt Lute and Borderless Press are not signs of a new knowledge economy. The need for presses like Borderless Press are indications of how racist and closed the dominant knowledge economy is with no desire to include excluded voices or even recognize that some voices are always silent. These independent presses are interventions. Aunt Lute publishes women of color and Borderless Press publishes scholars in Africa, Asia and South America, often publishing their first book after the completion of their PhD.

Our interventions need to be complemented by *knowledge activism* praxis that expands the one-off independent press interventions into a global *knowledge activism* movement that transforms the colonial knowledge economy into the decolonized knowledge economy. Like the system ignored the authors so the system also ignores interventionist publishers. The knowledge economy must change in order to claim that societies are postcolonial, that indeed we live in a period after colonialism. We can throw around words to describe the period after colonialism and if critique has moved from the temporal, but when the theoretical dust settles the dominant colonial knowledge system remains in place undisturbed.

---

for a New Age," *The Masalai Blog*, February 11, 2009, accessed October 6 2016, https://masalai.wordpress.com/2009/02/11/majority-world-a-new-word-for-a-new-age/.

There is no hands-off way to change the ecosystem through more elegant words and new theories. Nothing less than *knowledge activism* with a *knowledge activist* mindset will bring the systemic change necessary. The strength of activism and activist actions needs to put pressure on the various places in the ecosystem where there are no longer flows of knowledge. Public protests and annoying challenges to those with knowledge power will begin the necessary shifts. For example, *The Guardian* reported on September 6, 2016 that, "At Oxford, the Rhodes Must Fall campaign has become the spearhead of the movement to decolonize the university. The movement asks the university to confront its role in ongoing physical and ideological violence of empire."[2] Black and minority ethnic MA and PhD students are leading the movement at Oxford University.

We at Postcolonial Networks offer more than Borderless Press for another group of excluded authors in an ever-expanding genre of independent presses that have published marginalized authors over the last century. In this book we bring scholarship, publishing and activism together in order to promote decolonizing *knowledge activism*. Only when we combine our *knowledge activism* resources and mindsets will we sufficiently disrupt the dominant system flows.

Due to advances in technology and shift in economic patterns, the *knowledge system* is poised for change. The success of activism is due to calculated resistance efforts.

The only way these economic shifts will benefit marginalized and excluded authors is when all of us as knowledge activists accept our role in the bringing about of a new

---

[2] Neha Shah, "How Britain's Old Empire Lives on in Universities," *Guardian* (Online), September 6, 2016, accessed October 4 2016, https://www.theguardian.com/education/2016/sep/06/how-britains-old-empire-lives-on-in-universities.

knowledge economy. As you read this book we hope you will be clothed with the necessary *knowledge activist* mindset so that you will have an impact on this important work.

R.S. Wafula & Joseph F. Duggan

I. *KNOWLEDGE ACTIVISM*

Joseph F. Duggan

A. Why this Book Matters

James Cone wrote his prophetic *Black Theology and Black Power* in 1967.[1] In his short monumental work he called on white people to do their work. Four decades later several white scholars wrote the first book that responded to Cone's critique. Cone had been virtually ignored and quietly dismissed as white racism perpetuated throughout the academy and every American institution without any self-reflection, accountability, engagement or effort to change. Cone's activist writings were ignored for generations. Over three decades after Cone's work, in their book *Disrupting White Supremacy from Within: White People On What We Need To Do*, Jennifer Harvey, Karin Case and Robin Gorsline, three white scholars were the first to accept Cone's invitation and engage his criticism in 2008, forty-one years later.[2]

Ngũgĩ Wa Thiong'o wrote *The Decolonized Mind: The Politics of Language in African Literature* in 1997 where he

---

1. J. Cone, *Black Theology and Black Power*, (Maryknoll, NY: Orbis Books, 1967).

2. James Harvey, K. Case and Robert Gorsline, *Dismantling White Supremacy from Within: White People On What We Need To Do*, (Cleveland, OH: The Pilgrim Press, 2008).

critiqued Western systems of knowledge.[3] Ngũgĩ's work has been cited almost three thousand times in books and journals throughout the world. While Wa Thiong'o's work has been widely cited, there has been little reform in the academy to respond to his criticism that "English has not been rejected as a symbol of Colonialism."[4] It is not uncommon to avoid testimonies and critiques of Western knowledge systems as the silently convicted avoid self-reflection on their own privilege and biases that perpetuate imbalance of voice and power.

The Western academy including academic publishers lacks empathy when those it has marginalized speak up and describe their agony. When the members of the academy don't want to know, they close their eyes, ears and hearts to resist any changes that might open up opportunities for transformation. Both unconscious and conscious knowledge imperialism perpetuates the dominance of Western knowledge by the unquestioning practices of aspiring scholars, PhD candidates, teaching faculty, publishers, distributors, librarians and readers as well.

There is widespread naïveté in the academy that scholars without their PhD have no authority to speak in order to influence changes in the dominant system of knowledge as they patiently and submissively await approval of their "master" doctoral committee members. A number of years ago, Gloria Anzaldúa had a knowledge activist mindset when she published her first book, *Borderlands/La Frontera: The New Mestiza* in 1987 although she never completed her PhD. When she died in 2004 she was finishing her dissertation for the completion of her PhD requirements

---

3. Ngũgĩ Wa Thiong'o, *Decolonizing the Mind: The Politics of Language in African Literature* (Nairobi: EAEP, 1986).

4. Thiong'o, 31.

at the University of California Santa Cruz. Her PhD degree was awarded in 2005 posthumously.[5] Indeed, Anzaldua's groundbreaking book was cited in hundreds of other doctoral dissertations long before Anzaldua contemplated graduate school![6]

Several years ago a doctoral student submitted an abstract for a Postcolonial Networks conference to take place in South America. The abstract demonstrated significant promise for a great paper that would have been eventually published. When the young scholar's doctoral chair heard that her student's paper was accepted, the chair discouraged and even forbade *her* doctoral student from attending the meeting. The doctoral student accepted her doctoral chair's demand without question. Another woman wrote an abstract for the same meeting with a radical, queering of the trinity, but even though she was going to write with a pen name she was afraid that her faith-based university, if they found out, might not grant her tenure. Both women bowed out of their radical visions due to their institutional demands because they desired their doctorate and tenure respectively. And yet when the PhD is granted or tenure is awarded there seems to be often a lack of correlation with the unleashing and liberation of voice that disrupts knowledge and subverts the system that so routinely suppresses voices.

Marginalized scholars like these do not suddenly become *knowledge activists*. The Anzalduan effect is lost when newly minted PhD's, who eventually become an Assistant Professor or even the tenured Associate Professor, lack the

---

5. Gloria Anzaldúa, *Borderlands/La Frontera: The New Mestiza*, (San Francisco, CA: Aunt Lute, 1987).

6. However, the acceptance of Anzaldúa's work prior to her finishing her PhD is an exception rather than the rule as the next paragraph shows.

knowledge activist mindset to liberate their students' voices and that of their own. These dominant knowledge machine biases are the systems out of which the same biases are fostered that look down on Majority World scholars and their contributions. Several years ago when I was doing preliminary research for my series proposal to Palgrave for *Postcolonialism and Religions*, several senior faculty told me that I was wasting my time and that I would never find quality Majority World scholars to publish books. One respected professor told me 'they don't know how to write, they lack referencing and citation discipline, so you are wasting your time". Another professor told me that his department no longer accepts international students for his institution's doctoral programs because of their bad experiences with these students.

The colonial knowledge machine does not recognize geographical boundaries of North America and Europe. The colonial epistemological silencing effects continue throughout Majority World contexts. The colonial masters demeaned indigenous knowledge so that in post-independence years many libraries lacked the funds to adequately secure resources. In too many Majority World university classrooms, the professor is the only person in the room with a book and he/she reads, interprets and tells his/her students what they need to know. Even when quality books are available, there is a common custom to buy one book and copy for many others. Newly minted PhD's that seek to publish send their manuscripts to North American and European publishing houses, but often these projects are ignored or sent back for unreasonable and substantial revisions. One African scholar told me that a German publishing house said that his book would not be published unless he changed his research methodology from his local, indigenous source to Jurgen Habermas!

Demeaned and dispirited Majority World scholars then allow their manuscripts to go unpublished or are satisfied to have their book printed in exchange for payment to local "publishing" houses that follow none of the academic conventions that lead to valued knowledge and citations in other works. Where is value in the colonial knowledge machine and who evaluates knowledge to determine its value? This is a difficult question that easily enters circular cycles of silence that never emerge unless we push decolonial and postcolonial critical theories towards *knowledge activist* mindsets that actively transform the entire knowledge system author by author. In this book R.S. Wafula and I seek to unveil the annihilation of Majority World voices and all scholarship every time, every day another doctoral dissertation is approved lacking any Majority World citations!

About a year ago I was having lunch in New York with Burke Gerstenschlager, formerly an editor at Palgrave MacMillan. I was telling Burke of the challenges of finding funding for our knowledge activism work and the struggle to sustain our Postcolonial Networks' *knowledge activism* mission and commitment to publish Majority World scholars in Africa, Asia and South America through Borderless Press. I was explaining the way then I was working extra jobs to expand our small base of donors' impact and continue to accept Majority World authors' manuscripts for mentoring and eventual publication. Wafula was postponing payment of family debt to do this work too.

Gerstenschlager suggested that Postcolonial Networks and Borderless Press see knowledge activism as a vocation. He said and I paraphrase that the vocation of the *knowledge activist* is to take on those structural questions and struggles that the institutional academic and leading publishers do not yet systematically recognize as important or are most often completely out of view, invisible to these institutions' survival concerns. The *knowledge activist* persistently and often even annoyingly brings these questions and struggles to the attention of scholars, publishers and readers. *Knowledge activists* need to be as patient as they are determined to accompany the necessary awakening of centuries of conscious and unconscious knowledge imperialism with lack of awareness of the victims and victors of privilege.

Knowledge activists disrupt the normal state of epistemological affairs as they raise questions about inconsistencies that marginalize the voices of many for the benefit of a privileged few. Gerstenschlager said that *knowledge activists* like most activists ought not to expect to be compensated or celebrated, for they ask questions that established knowledge-based institutions cannot yet ask of themselves as their metrics of success make it impossible to lead the necessary changes. He went on to encourage me, in whatever necessary way, to nurture our *knowledge activist* communities, as the journey would be long before there were significant breakthroughs, but every *knowledge activist* action is a small contributing factor to the epistemological revolution that decolonizes knowledge beyond mere utterance of theories. Gerstenschlager's encouragement and conversations with Wafula have inspired us to write this book.

If knowledge-based institutions saw the needs and also the accompanying solutions that *knowledge activists* see there would be no need for *knowledge activists* or a knowledge-activist mindset. *Knowledge activism* necessarily happens on the outside of mainstream institutions on the periphery where one without anybody's permission has the agency, autonomy, authority and self-abandonment to ask the most difficult and challenging questions without fear of loss of prestige, privilege or other benefits such as not being approved for tenure. *Knowledge activism* also happens at the center of the knowledge economy in institutions too, but often at even higher personal costs as noted above.

On several occasions when I was writing for peer review journals, senior scholars mentored me to temper my critiques of other scholars and rather build upon and expand their arguments. The silencing of rigorous scholarly critiques has fostered a culture of theoretical avoidance that domesticates scholarship to serve the insular needs of small, privileged networks within the academy. Whereas Wafula and I were mentored to temper our voice, critique and rein in our visions, we have come together to promote and foster *knowledge activism* so that all people may reflect on the colonial epistemological impact that influences the way questions, research, writing, publishing and reading practices are performed. In the Appendix we have provided some questions to scholars, publishers, librarians and readers to initiate a pattern of self-reflection and change.

In this book we outline *knowledge activism* praxis after theory and how we can all take on the work of subverting the dominant *knowledge activist* system. Knowledge is power. The creation, exchange and distribution of knowledge patterns reflect the flow, location and position of power. Potential *knowledge activists* are publishers, librarians, faculty, scholars, authors, copy editors, and readers who disrupt dominant, hegemonic, unidirectional knowledge flows that privilege Western scholarship. They alternatively facilitate a diversity of authors, a multiplicity of knowledge flows in multiple directions in ways that engage a multiplicity of peoples, cultures, languages, narratives, methodologies and expressions to share power that expand cultures of justice. *Knowledge activism* is a communal collective that addresses the power imbalances in knowledge creation, exchange and distribution in order that learners may benefit from a limitless diversity of ideas.

We hope this book upsets you enough to make different knowledge choices! Our book will be a success if you are upset enough to make very different choices about the way you publish your scholarship, invite Majority World scholars into collaboration, and exercise leadership for subversive change. Our book may compel you to leave the system because the dominant system will not reward you for the ways you subvert the dominant knowledge production system. If you are already outside the dominant knowledge production system, such as the increasing number of adjuncts hardly working at a decent wage or as an independent researcher, now is your opportunity to leverage your autonomy in ways that build a better system of knowledge where the decolonial theories you promote in writing become reality for those not yet given the privilege to write, publish, and read. For those who choose to stay in the system, you can help by supporting the work of Majority World scholars through the modification of your syllabi to include Majority World scholarship, requiring your masters and doctoral students to cite Majority World scholarship and encouraging your library to invest in Majority World scholarship. Together we must build the *knowledge activism* movement to decolonize knowledge.

B. An Abbreviated Colonial Knowledge Simulation

A Majority World Doctoral Researcher sits in their school library in any nation in Africa and seeks to find content to build a literature review for their masters or doctoral dissertation or thesis. For illustrative purposes let's use Postcolonial Networks' partner institution, St. Paul's University in Limuru, Kenya, 30 miles outside of Nairobi. The St. Paul's Library has limited library resources. Once the resources have been fully utilized and the researcher still needs more access to complete their literature review of available sources then they must look outside their home school library. Let's also assume that the researcher is seeking to build a literature review on postcolonial resources in liturgy and worship.

Postcolonial liturgy and worship is a limited area of research, so the researcher needs to choose if they have access to enough resources. With larger research questions there is a risk that the researcher will have access to only a fraction of the available research. Junior scholars in Majority World contexts all the time write to me for a copy of a Palgrave book and I have to refer them to World Cat. When I am asked by a Majority World scholar for a Borderless Press book, I offer to send the book for free but the shipping often costs $25–$50.00, making it prohibitive for our small not-for-profit organization to send many books.

Since the St. Paul's Library has a copy of each of the Palgrave Macmillan *Postcolonialism and Religions'* series, as the publisher offered these to the St. Paul's Library as a gift, the researcher will find Claudio Carvalhaes' book, *Liturgy in Postcolonial Perspectives: Only One is Holy*.[7] It is fortunate the St. Paul's Library has this book, as World Cat

---

7. Cláudio Carvalhaes, *Liturgy in postcolonial perspectives: only one is holy* (New York, NY: Palgrave, 2015).

indicates that the closest library with Carvalhaes' book is South Africa, Germany or Switzerland.

Similarly, gifts have been given to the St. Paul's Library through the international travels of professors who receive gifts of books. In this way Kwok Pui-Lan's *Postcolonial Imagination and Feminist Theology* is found in the library collection, so the researcher will have this important foundational work for their literature review.[8]

The researcher finds Michael Jagessar and Stephen Burns' *Christian Worship: Postcolonial Perspectives*, but the closest libraries with the book are in Switzerland, Germany and the Netherlands.[9] It is unlikely that St. Paul's Inter-Library loan will help as books are expensive to ship and most libraries cannot afford the shipping cost. The researcher is then offered the opportunity to buy the book at $143 from Barnes and Noble! The researcher often writes to the author to request a copy, or less directly inquires how they might find a copy for their research. The author typically has been given only a few review copies, and likely they are all gone.

Kwok Pui-Lan just came out with a new book, *Postcolonial Practice of Ministry*: *Leadership, Liturgy, and Interfaith Engagement*.[10] It is possible that this book may eventually get to the St. Paul's Library through a gift. In the meantime, our researcher in Kenya finds that the book is available through several databases and can be read online. The book is available at EBSCOhost, lib.mylibrary.com and EBook Library. EBSCO and lib.mylibrary are accessible through Ath-

---

8. Kwok Pui-Lan, *Postcolonial Imagination and Feminist Theology*, (Louisville, KY: Westminster John Knox Press, 2005).

9. Michael N. Jagessar and Stephen Burns, *Christian Worship: Postcolonial Perspectives* (London: Routledge, 2014).

10. Kwok Pui-lan and S. Burns, *Postcolonial Practice of Ministry: Leadership, Liturgy, and Interfaith Engagement* (Lanham, MD: Lexington Books, 2016).

ens. The researcher goes to the St. Paul's Library website to see if they have access to Athens, and they do not. EBook Library looks like an option as it shows a PDF is available for download, but St. Paul's Library does not have access to this database. EBook Library is not a free service.

Postcolonial Practice of Ministry is too new a book to be available in the Library of Congress or the New York Public Library; neither is the 2014 book *Christian Worship* by Jagessar and Burns available. If either book was available, the researcher would have access to the full table of contents and a brief narrative summary of the book. The researcher sees a 2009 book by James K.A. Smith, *Desiring the Kingdom, Worship, Worldview, and Cultural Formation* and that it is available in electronic form.[11] Unfortunately, the New York Public Library is only available to those who live in New York City or New York State. It does provide a temporary library card to those out of state, but one needs to pick up the library card in person. The researcher is left with a scarce summary of the book and if the researcher eventually publishes a book with this limited information, the double-blind peer reviewer will challenge the author for their lack of critical analysis of the Smith book.

Returning to the World Cat, the researcher's search on "postcolonial, worship and liturgy" generates eight results. The Jagessar and Carvalhaes books are two of the eight results. A new researcher might be inclined to think that these two books make up the field of available research. A review of the Hollis Catalog generates sixteen results, but a review of the bibliographies of both the Jagessar and Carvalhaes books would generate far more leads on books and journal articles that the researcher would need to locate in

---

11. James K. A. Smith, *Desiring the Kingdom, Worship, Worldview, and Cultural Formation* (Grand Rapids, MI: Baker Academic, 2009).

their library at St. Paul's or a library within Kenya. While reviewing the search results, the researcher finds at the Union Seminary Library online, a journal article, "Kingdom Play? Striving Against Racisms through Worship in a Postcolonial Mode" published in the journal *Liturgy* and available through Taylor and Francis online.[12] St. Paul's has a subscription to the Taylor and Francis online database, so the researcher will be able to read this article.

The researcher will find many university libraries that offer online search access of their catalogs. Among these libraries is a small sample:

>Brown University
>
>Columbia University — CLIO search; partial results without password
>
>Cornell
>
>Dartmouth — catalog
>
>Harvard Hollis Search Catalog

National University of Singapore — has excellent abstracts on numerous books; an extensive postcolonial collection; 1600+ entries on decolonial and at the same time like all other libraries the fine print states that "due to licensing agreement regulations" non-members have no access to online resources.

>Yale University
>
>Oxford University Press
>
>Princeton
>
>St. Andrews University Scotland
>
>Stanford Search Works

---

12. Richard E. McCarron, "Kingdom Play? Striving Against Racisms through Worship in a Postcolonial Mode," *Liturgy*, 7 (2014): 47–54.

Trinity College Dublin Library

University of Central Florida

University of Hyderabad, India

University of Manchester, UK

University of Melbourne, Australia

University of Pennsylvania

University of Texas

There are many more universities that do not offer online access to their library resources. Some of these libraries include: Xavier University in Ohio and University of Wales.

The British, in celebration of the eight hundredth anniversary of the Magna Carta, invited all on the World Wide Web to vote on five hundred clauses submitted by three thousand young people across the world to create a new Magna Carta for the digital age.[13] The top ten clauses selected for "the web we want will":

1. Not let companies pay to control it and not let governments restrict our right to information.
2. Allow freedom of speech.
3. Be free of government censors in all countries.
4. Not allow any kind of government censorship.
5. Be available for all those who wish to use it.
6. Be free of censorship and mass surveillance.
7. Allow equal access to knowledge, information and current news worldwide.

---

13. Website of the British Library, "Magna Carta for the digital age 2015," *My Digital Rights Project,* June 15, 2015, accessed September 10 2016, http://www.bl.uk/my-digital-rights/magna-carta-2015.

8. Have freedom of speech.

9. Not be censored by the government.

10. Not sell our personal information and preferences for money, and will make it clearer if the Company Website intends to do so.

The British Library access to online resources is very limited. Most of the collections are Library-subscribed and are only available at British Library workstations.

Other challenges the researcher in Majority World-contexts encounters:

When the researcher is on campus they have access to the online catalog. The Library offers remote access, but students who live in local villages or far from school have limited Wi-Fi capabilities. Later in their publishing careers, those without regular Wi-Fi access face major challenges in making corrections post-double-blind peer review.

The intricacies of online search and the ways knowledge has been protected to serve the economic interests of subscription services, publishers and other information companies has been illustrated in this simulation. Colonial knowledge exists from the eyes of the Majority World researcher as he/she surfs the internet looking for relevant literature for their thesis and or dissertation. Beyond the journal databases of the home school library, when the researcher finds JSTOR content they will need to pay to access that content. Researchers in Kenya do not have the funds to access this restricted content.

The Majority World researcher encounters severe constraints and quickly sees where most knowledge resides and that one needs to be privileged to access it. *Knowledge activism* recognizes the perpetuation of dominant colonial knowledge-based systems that continue to privilege a few.

Knowledge activism makes public and visible these inequities in ways that challenge, disrupt and ultimately change the system.

C. Other Researchers in North America and Europe

In contrast the Minority World researcher-scholar-author in North America or Europe and every other privileged knowledge location has every book and journal article available to them in their school library, through Inter-Library Loans or through subscription services like JSTOR. Lack of research access is not a challenge that these researchers have due to their current methodological approach to research and writing. If, however, researchers were to aggressively seek Majority World scholarship for inclusion in their Minority World arguments they would be quickly met by the absence and lack of immediate availability of research online or in their home libraries. Robert Heaney, author of *From Historical to Critical Post-Colonial Theology: The Contribution of John S. Mbiti and Jesse N. K. Mugambi*, when he was doing his doctoral research at Oxford University travelled to Kenya to obtain resources for his research.[14] Few researchers like Heaney travel to the Majority World to find primary sources. More typically Minority World researchers travel to the Majority World on fellowships and grants to do ethnographic research that does not engage local communities and scholars.

One of the major differentiators between a Majority World research-writing style and a Minority World research-writing style is the kind of "isolation" the researcher-scholar writing experiences. The Majority World scholar is deeply

---

14. R. Heaney, *From Historical to Critical Post-Colonial Theology: The Contribution of John S. Mbiti and Jesse N. K. Mugambi* (Eugene, OR: Pickwick Publications, 2016).

immersed in their community as Wafula writes later, in this book, and at the same time is isolated from abundant scholarly resources. These impediments compromise the scholar's argument and eventual contribution to scholarship as double-blind peer reviewers and publishers reject their incomplete, under-researched manuscript. The Majority World author does not stand within his/her community set apart from other communities and nations. Although when the Majority World author brings in scholarship from other nations — especially North American and European scholars — it is often conflicted by layers of colonial narratives and relationships. While these narratives and relationships cannot be set aside, the Majority World author has not isolated herself/himself from others even when conflicted. Whereas the Minority World scholar often makes no effort to engage Majority World scholarship even when it is available.

II. EPISTEMOLOGICAL PRINCIPLES FOR *KNOWLEDGE ACTIVISM*

R.S. Wafula

A. Mapping Colonial Knowledge Systems

If you want to kill or marginalize people, you tell a story — a story of how the world is so much better without them. On the other hand, if you want to save people you also tell a story — a story of how the world is so much worse without them. It is instrumental to know that knowledge is passed on through stories. And these stories can either create life or destroy life. In this book we show both perspectives. We show how stories of colonial Euro-American epistemological systems have created epistemological death and marginalization of Majority World scholarship. But we also tell a story of how the world is so much worse without these Majority World knowledges (voices) in the academic cycles and in the process advocate for an accelerated production, distribution, and consumption of these neglected knowledges.

In order to understand the current status of knowledge production, consumption, and distribution in the world (and hence the life story we have chosen to tell) we need to understand the science of colonial knowledge processes.

In *Orientalism*, Edward Said defines orientalism as a Western discourse that represented non-Western peoples as different — as the "Other."[15] This Otherness is depicted in binary contrasts. The Orient is seen as an inferior place inhabited by intellectually inferior peoples, contrasted with the Europeans who are depicted as superior. Whereas oriental people are depicted as irrational, slow thinkers, inaccurate in their intellectual propositions, unreasonable, and illogical — at best representing anarchy and chaos, the European, in contrast, is depicted as rational, logical, and intelligent in all their dealings — the very embodiment of order and civility.[16] This ideology was purposely natured and developed through supporting institutions, vocabulary, scholarship, imagery, doctrines, colonial bureaucracies, and colonial styles. It was also supported by concerted efforts of Western scientists, scholars, missionaries, traders, and soldiers whose narratives depicted the so-called oriental people as a group of people whose inferiority had no redemption without European intervention.[17]

From Said's analysis one can deduce the sustained effort to represent not only oriental knowledge, but oriental people as primitive and backward. This primitiveness demarcates their epistemological systems as useless in the imagined European epistemological world. European knowledge is therefore marketed as the lifeline for the survival of Oriental people. But in order for the regeneration of oriental people to take place, the European epistemological framework, supported by well calculated and heavily funded machinery, calls for the erasure of oriental

---

15. Edward W. Said, *Orientalism* (New York, NY: Vintage Books, 1978), 2.
16. Ibid. 38.
17. Ibid. 7.

knowledge systems and their replacement with European epistemological systems.

Walter Mignolo points out that the above binary perspective was passed on as unqualified truth.[18] With such overwhelming power, machinery, and resources, the West constructed what it purported to be as all there is to know about oriental peoples. As V.Y. Mudimbe points out, this construction of the Other was no mean narrative. It constituted a body of knowledge that has governed Western understanding of the Other for generations.[19] As a result, what orientalism (the creation of Oriental people) did was not only to deprive the Oriental people the right to represent themselves, but also the legitimacy to be heard should they ever represent themselves. This twin agenda was then calculatedly filtered into all fields of academic discourses (biology, geography, history, sociology, anthropology, linguistics, religious/theology, and so forth) and sociopolitical and economic systems. The combined bodies of knowledge marketed the idea that the Other is incapable of self-government, self-determination, self-advancement, and self-representation — that everything they do is doomed to fail.[20] Thus in the process of knowledge production, distribution, and consumption, the European epistemological frameworks practiced what Paulo Freire calls "the banking concept" of education. The "teacher," in this case the European, possessing all knowledge deposits it in the empty bank account (the head of the student). Thus the student is perceived as an empty vessel with no intelligence. As a

---

18. Walter D. Mignolo, *Local Histories/Global Designs: Coloniality, Subaltern Knowledges, and Border Thinking* (Princeton, NJ: Princeton University Press, 2000), ix.

19. V.Y. Mudimbe, *The Invention of Africa: Gnosis, Philosophy, and the Order of Knowledge* (London: James Curey, 1988), 1–16.

20. Said, *Orientalism*, 12, 32–34.

result, the nature of knowledge and its acquisition becomes a Euro-American gift to the Majority World peoples.[21]

The European perception of the Oriental people was not uniquely limited to the Middle Eastern peoples. Africans suffered the same fate. Mudimbe shows how European exploration, colonization, and imperialization of Africa granted them power to organize and transform Africa into a European construct. He shows how the idea of an "African" began to be organized around pictorial and textual images of Africa and Africans as primitive savages.[22] These images were in turn reinforced by European discourses on Africa through disciplines such as anthropology and biology.[23] Through these disciplines, Mudimbe points out that the Europeans developed an epistemological ethnocentrism whose premise was that scientifically speaking there is nothing that can be learned from primitive African "savages." The European became the guardian of all human history, developing an epistemological system of knowledge that claimed to be the guardian and sum of all knowledges.[24] Thus anything of intellectual value has to come from outside — namely from the Europeans.[25] Unfortunately this monolithic Eurocentric claim has gone unchallenged for a very long time. The reason for this is explained by George J. Sefa Dei. Dei argues that for a long time historiography has privileged European history over Majority World Histories for the simple reason that the medium of historiography has been predominantly through written documentation.

---

21. Paulo Freire, *Pedagogy of the Oppressed*, 30th edition (London; New York, NY: Continuum, 2000), 71–72.

22. V.Y. Mudimbe, *The Idea of Africa* (Bloomington and Indianapolis, IN: Indiana University Press, 1994), 1–36.

23. Mudimbe, *The Invention of Africa*, 1–9, 17

24. Mignolo, *Local Histories/Global* Design, x.

25. Mudimbe, *The Invention of Africa*, 15.

For over five hundred years, Europeans dominated written history at a time when much of Majority World histories (in the case of Dei, Africa) was passed on through the medium of oral historiography.[26] I would argue that the situation has not changed much. Knowledge in terms of written resources is heavily imbalanced against the Majority World. The production, distribution, and consumption of knowledge still privileges Euro-American writings over Majority World writings.

Both Said and Mudimbe point out how this historiography in the post–active colonization period was carried out through the nineteenth- and twentieth-century mushrooming academic centers around the Western world purportedly dedicated to the "objective" and "scientific" study of African and Oriental studies, among others. According to Mudimbe, these centers, particularly Western-oriented anthropology, became the "ancestor" of colonial narratives, fronting an epistemological determinism based on the binary category that Europeans are academically superior to Africans in every way.[27] Thus Africa can only be understood through the eyes of a European and in terms of comparative negation to superior Europe. According to the Euro-American narratives, Africa does not have proper attributes of human nature (read: European nature). Africa is "all that is incomplete, mutilated, and unfinished ... absolute otherness ... the very figure of the strange."[28]

The philosophies behind the above studies coupled with the historical Darwinian theories of human development

---

26. George J. Sefa Dei, *Teaching Africa: Towards a Transgressive Pedagogy* (New York, NY: Springer Publishers, 2012), 1–3.

27. Said, *Orientalism*, 45–55; Mudimbe, *The Invention of Africa*, 20–23, 44–72; *The Idea of Africa*, 38.

28. Achille Mbembe, *On the Postcolony* (Berkeley, CA: University of California Press, 2001), 1–3.

continue to govern policies for knowledge production, distribution, and consumption to date. They continue to support the prevailing understanding in the West that nothing academically important can come from non-Western countries because the inhabitants of these places are academically inferior — that the world misses nothing if there is no knowledge production by peoples from Majority World contexts. Chinua Achebe reflects on this issue in his experiential encounter with critics of his writings. In his book, *Home and Exile,* he shows how a British critic evaluated his novel, *Things Fall Apart* as a primitive anarchic voice against the orderly British imperial rule.[29] Achebe argues that this critique simply follows a tradition of British writing that consistently evaluated Africans as not only primitive but the very negation of human decency.[30] It was then that Achebe says he understood the absolute power of storytelling and that those who secure this privilege can arrange stories about others pretty much where, and as, they like.[31] Thus Achebe's writing is an effort to reclaim this power — a wrestling to get it out of imperial hands and placing it in the hands of the Africans who can describe themselves on their own terms. He had a sense of "divine duty" to tell his own story about himself, his people and his country.[32] Adding a voice to this call, Dei states that as Africans "we must reclaim and affirm our past intellectual traditions, knowledge, and contributions to world history as a necessary exercise in our decolonization" process.[33] It is this urgency to let the Majority voices tell their own

---

29. Chinua Achebe, *Home and Exile* (New York, NY: Anchor Books, 2000), 99.
30. Ibid., 29–35.
31. Ibid., 24.
32. Ibid., 37–72.
33. Dei, *Teaching Africa*, 6.

stories alongside other academic stories that is behind the writing of this book. Ours is not just an academic exercise, but an exercise of decolonization through knowledge production, distribution, and consumption of Majority World knowledges alongside all other knowledges from around the world.

There is also a prevailing understanding in Euro-American circles that Western scholars have sufficiently written or known enough about Africa and Africans that there is nothing new that inhabitants of these places can make known.[34] Pinning on this understanding, the whole knowledge production machinery from Western academicians to publishers has little interest in non-Western scholars and their scholarship. There are few Western scholars who engage in meaningful collaborative endeavors with non-Western scholars simply because they, consciously or unconsciously, buy into the narrative that they have nothing to gain by such collaborations. Publishers, for their part, often times reject manuscripts from non-Western scholars on the basis of not only marketability, but also on the fallacious assumption that Majority World scholars do not contribute substantially to "scholarship" as defined by Western standards. The resulting effect is that the knowledge machinery relationship is a train that heads one way full and returns empty. The West can send its scholars and its books to help Majority World scholars. But the Majority World has nothing to send back to the West — no books, no scholars, and no knowledge.[35]

---

34. One British colonial administrator in Said's *Orientalism* (31–34) states that the British know everything there is to know about Egypt. In other words, no Egyptians independent of British administrators know anything about themselves beyond what these British people know.

35. Although a lot of brain drain takes place from Majority World places to Euro-American centers of academia, none of these scholars arrive as expatri-

Like Achebe, I came to the understanding of how the philosophy of the "one-way train" works experientially rather than through theoretical knowledge. My first academic journey out of Kenya took me to Edinburgh University in Scotland. In one of my classes a professor commended, "I am surprised that you have come here to do biblical studies. Most Africans come here into the program of 'Society and Culture.' Biblical studies is serious business." At first I took his words as a compliment. But much later I realized the implications of what he meant. By comparing biblical studies to society and culture studies in the framework of "most Africans" versus European students, the learned professor was implying that Africans are academically inferior and could not do biblical studies. According to him they could only do much less academically demanding programs such as culture and society studies (I doubt that scholars in this specialty would have agreed with the learned professor that theirs was a less academically demanding program. It is like comparing oranges to mangoes).[36]

My second academic journey took me to the USA where I went through two other master's programs before completing a PhD. Throughout these graduate years, I received generous academic scholarships. However, these scholarships were given primarily as bait as part of the fundraising efforts of the colleges — of showing the donors that the

---

ates in the sense of Euro-American "experts" arriving in Majority World contexts. They rather arrive as "refugee" scholars and hence join a host of other minoritized scholars in the Euro-American academia fighting every day to prove that they are scholars worth their title.

36. Of course the work of Knut Holter "Sub-Saharan African Doctoral Dissertations in Old Testament Studies, 1967–2000: Some Remarks to their Chronology and Geography," in *Biblical Interpretation in African Perspective* (ed. David Tuesday Adamo; Lanham, Maryland: University Press of America, 2006), and my own journey that culminated in becoming a PhD holder would disapprove the assertions of my learned professor.

colleges support helpless Africans. The idea of supporting a potential African scholar who can contribute to Euro-American epistemological advancement or to world knowledge had no place in the colleges' mission statements. As part of my scholarships I was invited to fundraising meetings with potential donors and made to tell a story of myself as a poor African who is being saved by "a white man's college." Thus I was paraded as a token to solicit more money for other future poor Africans. I felt the same experience in most of my classes where I was perceived as a recipient of Western ideas and education rather than a "diversity graduate student" who has some unique African perspective that could enrich the seminar discussions. I was also surprised at the selection of reading materials for most of my courses. Even when some of the programs I went through had a significant number of students from the Majority World, most of the books that were assigned for the courses were all written by Western academicians. I realized that the American education system feeds, consciously or unconsciously, into the very same idea that nothing of academic value can be gained from the Majority World.

Unfortunately, the above view is not restricted to higher education. I have since been educated by my first-year undergraduate American students that they hardly learned much African history or geography in their elementary and high schools. As a way of introducing myself to my students, I often tell them the story of myself as a Kenyan. I would then ask them trivia questions about Kenya and Africa. Many of these students were unable to answer simple geographical questions such as capital cities of African countries or approximate geographical location of certain African countries on the African continent. This problem is a double tragedy. On the one hand the African scholars and scholarship are denied a chance to tell the world of the wonderful wealth of knowledge that Africa can bring into the academic world. But on the other hand, the Western world becomes progressively illiterate of what goes in the non-Western world. Something has to be done to address this double tragedy. We need concerted efforts to contest colonial knowledge systems that deny the world the richness of world knowledges by restricting knowledge to Euro-American knowledge.

B. Contesting Colonial Knowledge Systems

Contesting colonial knowledge systems is an enterprise that is gaining momentum in academia — almost becoming an academic subfield of its own. One of the groundbreaking works in this area has been done by Walter D. Mignolo. Mignolo makes an argument that the present knowledge system is based on what he calls the "colonial difference" where the knowledges of all other peoples are subordinated to European epistemological principles of superiority. He points out, for example, how Ancient Eastern scientific knowledge would be classified as mysticism while European knowledge would be classified as modern physics, even when both may have logical scientific sophistication.[37] In order to counter this difference he proposes blurring the boundaries between Eurocentric and *Othered* systems of knowledge. According to him this can be done by enacting what he calls "border thinking." Border thinking privileges subaltern knowledge (local histories) by not only bringing these knowledge systems to light, but also by discussing and exposing the fallacies of colonial difference that submerge such knowledge.[38] This process, according

---
37. Mignolo, *Local Histories/Global designs*, 6.
38. Ibid, 9, 20–22.

to Mignolo, would lead to a "multiplicity of epistemic energies in diverse local histories" in the evolving process of rearticulating global epistemological designs.[39] In other words in the very Western *subaltening* of the Other lies the impetus for subaltern resistance located in border thinking between *subalterned* identities and colonial epistemologies.[40] Mignolo concludes that border thinking allows for the celebration of Western knowledge and other knowledges without superiority/inferiority binarisms. It moves beyond eurocentrism by recognizing and valuing non-Western systems of knowledge in equal measure to other knowledges.[41] Thus epistemological knowledge decoloniality resides in seeking to eliminate dichotomies that privilege Western knowledge from Other knowledges.[42] Mignolo's theory is very fascinating. However, it needs follow-up work that would enact actual praxes to remedy the colonial differencing of knowledge that he so eloquently describes. We consider the proposals in this book as one alternative for addressing the problem that Mignolo raises.

Another critical voice against Euro-American epistemological racism is that of Sandy Grande. Grande stands up against the marginalization of Native Americans knowledge systems — of what she calls Red Pedagogy. Her first shot against this knowledge imperialism is fired against the twin alliance of Church and state against Native Americans. She argues that "the church and the state have acted as coconspirators in the theft of Native America, robbing

---

39. Ibid., 39.
40. Ibid., 84–88.
41. Ibid., 319.
42. Ibid., 337.

indigenous peoples of their right to be indigenous."[43] According to her, this thievery began by French Jesuits in 1611. They in turn were closely followed by the Spanish and British missionaries. These groups destroyed Native American knowledge systems in the name of "civilizing" and "Christianizing" Native American peoples all the while advancing white supremacy. Over the years, part of this process involved establishing boarding schools where young Native American children were yanked away from their homes for long periods each year and indoctrinated with epistemological frameworks that projected Native American education and culture as primitive compared to European culture. The boarding schools were meant to extinguish Indian-ness by introducing the Indian children to imperialistic Eurocentric epistemologies. However Grande points out that, in the late 1960s, many Indian groups formed organizations to fight for their emancipation.[44] Although gains have been made since the 1960s to the present, many Native Americans lag behind in education and all sociopolitical and economic processes in the US. In order to decolonize not only the Native Indian education systems, but the Native Indian lives, Grande proposes that society must acknowledge not only the relationship between education and culture, but also the relationship between culture and socioeconomic conditions of Native Indians. This is because, for her, American-engineered Indian education was not simply meant to "civilize" the Indian, but it was a project meant to colonize Indian minds as a means of gaining access to free Indian labor, land, and resources. As such, a project to decolonize the mind through re-education

---

43. Sandy Grande, *Red Pedagogy: Native American Social and Political Thought* (Lanham, MD: Rowman & Littlefield Publishers, 2004), 11.

44. Ibid., 12–18, 27.

should go hand-in-hand with combating the forces of colonialism in all their manifestations.[45] This project should be captured by a critical pedagogy that combines theory and praxis with emancipation as its primary end goal.[46] According to Grande, it is this emancipation coupled with hope in the beliefs and understandings of the ancestors and the power of traditional knowledge that would liberate and set Native Indians free.[47]

For Grande what stands between the Native Americans and their emancipatory goals is American government-engineered pedagogies sold as American democracy where in the name of nationalism, Native Indians are oppressed and denied the right to sovereignty and freedom. Nationalism (or nationhood) requires Native Indians to subscribe to unity under the nation-state. But the problem, as Grande notes, is that while the Native Indians are progressively forced to bring their lives into unison with the interests of the nation-state, hundreds of years of marginalization have already demarcated them as outsiders in the very nation-state that they are being called to be a part of. Thus the democracy of the nation-state does not serve their interests in the sense that Native Indians cannot participate in this democracy on equal footing as other races. Thus for Grande, the only hope for democracy is granting the Native Indians internal sovereignty within the nation-state.[48] This sovereignty, for Grande, does not pose any problem to nation-state democracy since it is not built on a power hierarchy. It simply grants the Native Indians the space to chart their destiny through empowering Native Indians

---

45. Ibid., 19.
46. Ibid., 27–28.
47. Ibid., 28–29.
48. Ibid., 32, 36–46.

for self-government, utilization of Native languages, and charting their own paths for economic growth, among other things.[49] This sovereignty is achieved through the dreams of what Grande calls "Red Pedagogy" which mediates between capitalistic pedagogies of Western civilization and democracy and revolutionary pedagogies grounded in Marxist policies. Red Pedagogy is grounded in the fact that there is no Native Indian past that can be salvaged in a romanticized manner, but that freedom for Native Indians must be continually sought in the changing experiences and sociopolitical and economic realities of the Native Indians in the US — in the fourth luminal spaces that invest power in the Native Indian epistemological frameworks.[50]

One must applaud Grande's succinct and sustained defense of Native American epistemological framework over and against the US imperial nation-state oppression and dispossession of Native Indians. In her closing remarks she sets forth the following declarations about Red Pedagogy: Red Pedagogy is the manifestation of sovereignty, engaging the development of "community-based power," a power that articulates the recovery, reimagination, and reinvention of indigenous ways of being. Red Pedagogy implores conversations about power to include the examinations of responsibility and collective actions. Red Pedagogy embraces an educative process that works to reenchant the universe, to reconnect peoples to the land, and it is as much about belief and acquiescence as it is about questioning and empowering the Native Indians.[51] I must say that these are wonderful declarations. However, Grande does not answer the "how, who, what, when, where" questions of her

---
49. Ibid., 53–56.
50. Ibid., 166.
51. Ibid., 167–170.

proposals. Who is to shoulder the responsibility of rolling out the praxes that would enact Native Indian emancipation? How does that roll-out look? What are the programs that would actualize the epistemological deliverance of Native Indian knowledges? The answers to these questions are inevitably unavoidable if a viable program for real practical changes have to be carried out. Although Grande gives some historical developments in the Indian education emancipation, she does not offer a full-fledged praxis that would answer the questions raised above. Whereas she critiques Western epistemological frameworks for their abstractness and lack of praxes, her theorization does not break away from this same critique. In the latter parts of this book we provide one alternative that seeks to link theory to praxis by attending to questions of practices that can enhance epistemological justice.[52] In the meantime let us attend to other theorists against Euro-American epistemological colonialism.

Linda Tuhiwai Smith writes to contest Euro-American epistemological frameworks against the indigenous Maori people. The European immigrants to New Zealand demarcated the Maori as being primitive. They were a people who could not use their intellect to invent things, create history and institutions. They could not imagine or produce anything of value. As a result of imputing these negative characteristics on the Maori people, the Europeans were able to then argue that the very nature of the Maori people disqualified them from being human. The European epistemological framework arrogated upon itself the power to define what constitutes being human or

---

52. See also my essay, "What is Contextual Hermeneutics? Justin S. Ukpong and Beyond," in *The Postcolonial Church: Theology, Identity, and Mission* (eds., R.S. Wafula, Esther Mombo, and Joseph Wandera; Alameda, CA: Borderless Press, 2016), 93–107.

inhuman.[53] This classification of the Other was enhanced by the Enlightenment notions. With the Industrial Revolution, the increased European exploration of other lands and encounter of other peoples, and the need to support the European economy, the Europeans' imperial and colonial philosophies allowed them to 'see', 'name,' and 'know' the Other in ways that would support their imperial agendas. [54] By demarcating themselves as being human and the Maori as being inhuman, the Europeans found justification that granted them express right to take Maori land at will. But in order to entrench European superiority and colonization the Europeans used a colonial system of education to recruit Maori allies. Just like the European immigrants to the Americas did to the Native Americans, the Europeans in New Zealand used education as a tool to assimilate and co-opt Maori people into European culture. It caused the European-educated Maori to convert to European colonial ideals. These "educated" Maori were in turn given the teaching role to help bring other Maori people into the world of Western civilization. The "teachers," being closely aligned to European colonizer's tastes and class interests, repudiated their Maori education and values, even as their European creators hailed them as the saviors of their people.[55] Salvation therefore became a colonizing process that used divide and rule colonial strategy to further fracture the Maori people and erase their peoplehood.

Due to the negations of the humanity of the Maori people, Smith suggests that a decolonial project needs to involve programs aimed at reclaiming the lost humanity of the in-

---

53. Lind Tuhiwai Smith, *Decolonizing Methodologies: Research and Indigenous Peoples*, 2nd ed. (London & New York, NY: Otago University Press, 2012), 26.

54. Ibid., 62–63.

55. Ibid., 68–73.

digenous Maori peoples. One of the ways this can be done is to let the indigenous people write their own history and stories. This writing should not just be limited to telling the story, but should encompass also the right to research and theorize in ways that do not co-opt Euro-American epistemological frameworks to marginalize the indigenous people.[56] Smith points out that another strategy for the emancipation of Maori people has been organization of social movements for indigenous peoples to agitate for the rights of the Maori people — rights that range from land to education and to access to economic privileges. Since the 1960s the social movement has had a clear research agenda whose core is self-determination of Maori people. The agendas for social change included ideals such as decolonization, transformation, development, recovery, mobilization, and survival.[57] Smith points out that a number of Maori research programs have been initiated to articulate the above values.[58] In these research endeavors, the Maori people are asking their own questions and seeking their own answers, hence asserting the value of Maori knowledge as opposed to Euro-American epistemologies that had been imposed on the Maori people.

However, Smith's book is more descriptive, aimed more at theorizing how indigenous Maori people respond to their marginalization than providing her vision of the praxes that can be developed to emancipate Maori people from Eurocentric epistemologies. But her research is an eye-opener into what is happening among the Maori people that is instructive for practical projects that should be emulated among other marginalized communities. There

---

56. Ibid., 27, 36–41.
57. Ibid., 112–125.
58. Ibid., 127–142, 143–164.

is a need to empower Majority World peoples to engage in scholarly research, to produce their own knowledges, and to disseminate these knowledges for the benefit of the rest of the world of academia and in so doing enrich the world with the potential for human survival that lies latent in these continents.

From the African context, Ngũgĩ Wa Thiong'o starts his contest against colonial epistemologies of knowledge production, distribution, and consumption by an argument that the worst form of imperialism meted out on the African peoples was cultural imperialism — of what he calls a cultural bomb. According to him the cultural "bomb" destroys a people's faith in their own humanity to the extent that they long for something outside themselves to fill that void.[59] The genesis for the African cultural "bomb" has its roots in the Berlin conference of 1884. This all-European conference did not only politically divide Africa into bordered countries, but it also cultured Africa linguistically into English-speaking, French-speaking, German-speaking, or Portuguese-speaking countries. Over the course of colonization these languages became not just languages among others (African languages), but became "the" languages privileged over African languages. That would have been okay if language was just mere words. But Wa Thiong'o argues that language has power beyond just words. Language transmits cultural values which in turn produce a people's self-definition and history. Thus by effecting mental control through language, European countries were able to take control of the destiny of the whole realm of African lives.[60] Through these languages Europeans achieved a twin purpose of "destroying or undervaluing of African culture, art,

---

59. Wa Thiong'o, *Decolonizing the Mind*, 3.
60. Ibid., 9–16.

dances, religions, history, geography, education, orature, and literature, while elevating the sociocultural and political values of the colonizer.[61]

For Wa Thiong'o therefore, African renaissance lies in its capacity to reclaim its cultural values through the reintroduction of African languages in African educational institutions. The learning of African languages should begin the process of dislodging the prominence of European languages and hence transmit African cultural values in place of foreign imperial values.[62] To live up to his own vision, Wa Thiong'o began writing in his mother tongue (Gĩkũyũ), a gesture that he describes made him "abnormal" in academic circles. He argues that by adopting his mother tongue he had actually become "normal," but imperial reality had normalized English to the extent that normal is abnormal and abnormal is normal.[63] Wa Thiong'o therefore sees his role as one of helping restore the African to his/her rightful harmonious sociocultural life where the African can take charge of his/her own destiny.

One cannot help but admire Wa Thiong'o's ambitious proposal. He speaks for many of us when he states that we were forcefully and brutally uprooted from our languages and planted into foreign languages. It is sad that we, the victims of mental colonization, can speak and can express ourselves better in foreign languages than we can in our own mother tongues. For most of us this violent *re-languaging* came with a high cost. It came with the physical violence on our bodies. As for me I lost count of the number of times I was severely beaten in my primary (elementary) school for speaking my mother tongue in the

---

61. Ibid., 16.
62. Ibid., 26–27.
63. Ibid., 27–28.

confines of school compound rather than English. I sighed with relief when I finished primary school and went on to secondary school. Although there were no beatings in secondary school for failure to speak English, there was a different kind of tyranny. The syllabus required that I take, among other subjects, advanced classes in English. Without lessons in my mother tongue and being away in school most of the year, for the next six years English occupied a central place in my thought processes (and conversations) over my mother tongue. This primacy of English was to find its maturation in graduate school where I was made to sit French and German language exams as part of the brutal requirements for my PhD. I have nothing against learning languages. As a matter of fact, by being Kenyan-born I am a bilingual product. By the time I completed high school I could write and speak my mother tongue, English, and Kiswahili. But to insist, as most graduate programs do (at least in biblical studies in the USA) that all knowledge is epistemically bound up in three European languages (English, French, and German) is absurd. It underscores the continuing legacy of Eurocentrism sustaining Mignolo's idea that these European languages are not just a question of geography (Europe) but also about a function of epistemology — of imperial knowledge control of the Other.[64] Thus, in my case, the Other can become a biblical scholar only if they can master the formulations of Eurocentric epistemology.

Wa Thiong'o also speaks for many of us when he states that it is time for something to be done to restore what we have lost through resurrecting the learning of our African

---

64. Mignolo, *The Dark Side of Western Modernity: Global Futures, Decolonial Options* (Durham, NC: Duke University Press, 2011), 19.

languages, among other things.[65] But almost four decades since Wa Thiong'o made this proposal, foreign languages have continued to dominate African countries as official languages of government, education, and even commerce. What went wrong with Wa Thiong'o's vision? I suggest that among the contributory factors for the failure is the continued legacy of imperial dominance of the sociopolitical, economic, and educational processes of African countries. This continuation is supported by an African ruling elite who since independence have aligned their policies with their former colonizers for their political gain at the expense of the interests of their citizenry. As a result of this there was no goodwill sympathy for Wa Thiong'o proposal either at home or abroad. Hence Wa Thiong'o became a lone voice — a voice in the desert. But perhaps the other factor in the failure of Wa Thiong'o's decolonial project was lack of an acceptable praxiological plan for his decolonial theory. Once he started writing in his mother tongue, Wa Thiong'o together with his friends, developed a drama (theatre) group in Kamīrīīthū village near Limuru, Kenya (that came to be called Kamīrīīthū Community Education and Cultural Center) where his most famous play, translated in English as, "I will Marry When I Want" was performed in Gĩkũyũ.[66] Wa Thiong'o believed that change would be brought about by the peasantry — the people on the lowest social and economic ladder of society in Kenya who were hard hit by the effects of imperialism. But the play, being politically controversial, was banned by President Moi's dictatorial regime. Nothing else in terms of a practical plan was enacted by Wa Thiong'o, after that. In Kenyan political cycles he became a hunted down human being

---

65. Wa Thiong'o, *Decolonizing the Mind*, 27.
66. Written in collaboration with Ngũgĩ wa Mĩriĩ.

— eventually being forced into exile to save his dear life. Whereas Wa Thiong'o believed that change would require a revolution from the peasantry, history has shown that this is not enough — that decolonial change would require not only the concerted efforts of the victims but also of the victimizers as well. Both the colonizer and the colonized, to use Albert Memmi's words, must come to a point in their self-awareness where in the hermeneutics of the "face" (see next section), they can value human life above all other interests and work together for the common good.[67] This process would not be a single event, but a long history characterized by an intentional series of events informed by the idea that the whole world has a moral and ethical responsibility to right the imperial wrongs that were committed against Majority World peoples.

In terms of the English language, and unlike Wa Thiong'o, I do not advocate the erasure or minimization of English language from Kenyan communities.[68] Societies change

---

67. Albert Memmi, *The Colonizer and the Colonized* (Boston, MA: Beacon Press, 1991), xvii. Memmi makes a claim worth its salt that oppression is the greatest calamity of humanity since it destroys both the oppressed and the oppressor. It does not make the oppressor any safer (since the oppressor has now an enemy).

68. The contestation over the use of English is more volatile in South Africa where according to the 1996 constitution all the eleven official languages "must enjoy parity of esteem and be treated equitably." The bone of contention arises from the reality that English is used disproportionally over all the other ten languages in government, education, commerce, music, and even in informal settings. For the full story, see the article in *The Economist*, "South Africa's Languages: Tongues under Threat, English is Dangerously Dominant," January 20, 2011, accessed 1 April 2016, http://www.economist.com/node/17963285. My point is that this contestation and animosity against the English language would be minimized when we domesticate it and hence make it a hybridized African language as much as other African languages. This is of course not to minimize Ngũgĩ Wa Thiong'o's argument that language is a transmitter of not only words but sociocultural, political, and economic values, but to argue that there is limited room to undo its current utility. Cultures evolve and our African cultures have been shaped by colonial languages that we cannot wish away. We should rather, in the case of English, re-*englishcize* English through

and one of our African changes, negative as it may be, includes the effects of colonization and the production and utilization of English language among us. We cannot wish that away. In this sense English should be claimed as a Kenyan language just as any other Kenyan indigenous language. The difficulty of course is the Euro-American acceptance of *Kenyanized* English. This becomes evident whenever Kenyans (and for that matter all other Majority World peoples) leave Kenya for Britain or America. It is then that we become rudely made aware that our English is not English at all, or to be precise not "Standard English."[69] This is often stated in less conventional means. It often comes in the contexts of conversations where one is asked, "You have an accent, where do you come from?" Initially when I first heard these worlds, I thought they meant that I speak English with a strange variation and hence needed to explain my origin. By time, however, I came to know that the question was politically and racially loaded with demeaning nuances. An "accent" meant that I did not know how to speak "proper" English. My African "accent" was equivalent to defective English. Surprisingly this judgement does not apply to British or American "accent" English. Thus in general (to an American), a British accent sounds exotic and sweet to the ear. But an African accent sounds crude, hard to understand, and unintelligible even though an American would find challenges understanding both British and African English accents. Once you notice these differential treatments of people along language accents, you begin to realize that the binary divide is more about racial philosophies rather than mere linguistic ac-

---

natural processes such as creolization, or similar to Kiswahili evolvement (from African and Arabic languages).

69. *Standard* here refers to British and American English.

cent differences. Gloria Anzaldúa calls this racial linguistic differencing of people linguistic terrorism. She notes how *Chicanonized* Spanish or English is looked down upon as inferior, referring not so much on the inferiority of language, as it is on the inferiority of Chicano people in contrast to Spanish or English-speaking white Americans.[70]

This racialized linguistic differentiation is not limited to spoken English. It also applies to written English. Primacy and privilege is given to American or British conventions of writing English as the standard of how English language is deployed. Being originally from Kenya, and studying first in Scotland and then in the USA, I had to constantly worry about bringing my written English to "standard." Thus I have learned experientially the tyranny of Euro-American hegemonic English over me.[71] My most humiliating moments were in graduate school where I was constantly told to run my papers by an "English Expert" so that my writing can make proper sense to my professors. Once this suggestion was repeated again and again, it started affecting my self-image perceptions — that maybe I was not just good enough. Thus there is validity in Wa Thiong'o's argument that Western imperial standards make one lose faith in self and puts one on a path where one is constantly fighting to reclaim the 'self' from the abyss of inferiority.[72]

The irony of the matter is that whereas Euro-American epistemological frameworks are responsible for the dominant usage of English language among the Majority World people, Euro-Americans now reject the English spoken in the Majority World contexts. Having forcefully "planted"

---

70. Gloria Anzaldúa, *Borderlands/La Frontera: The New Mestiza* (San Francisco, CA: Aunt Lute Books, 1987), 75–86.

71. Cf. Mignolo, *Local Histories/Global Designs*, 4–5.

72. Wa Thiong'o, *Decolonizing the Mind*, 3.

English they now refuse to have that language "grow." They can't accept the inevitable idea that language evolves and mutates into different inflections across continents and time. If we can accept the idea that there is something called American or British English, or that there is something called archaic English in contrast to modern English, why would we not in the same vein accept the idea of African *Englishes* as contrasted to other forms of English?[73] Why, as Anzaldúa asks, would we have to accommodate the tastes of Euro-American speakers, rather than them accommodating us? Wanting not to delegitimize her language she insists on wanting to speak *Spanglish* rather than either "standard" Spanish or English.[74] The above questions are what the players in the machinery of knowledge production, distribution, and consumption need to answer. This is especially crucial for academic programs and publishers; two groups that are notoriously particular about standardizing English language to Euro-American tastes. We need to exercise what Dei calls epistemological equity where the knowledge of other people who are different from us is given an equal status — that we can work to tame our biases and exercise social responsibility and accountability to each other.[75] This will help us change the sorry status of competitive attitude which seeks to privilege one epistemological framework over another and also lead us to accept that difference is an unavoidable reality of humanity.

---

73. Timothy T. Ajani, in his article "Is There Indeed A "Nigerian English?", *JH & SS* 1:1 (2007): N.P. Accessed April 1, 2016 http://www.scientificjournals.org/journals2007/articles/1084.htm, argues for the validity of Nigerian English. In the article he concludes that "there is a preponderance of evidence for the existence of a Nigerian variety of English" that should be given equal status with other forms of *Englishes* spoken around the world.

74. Anzaldúa, *Borderlands/La Frontera*, 81.

75. Dei, *Teaching Africa*, 90.

Rather than see these differences as deficiencies, we need to view them as unknown knowledge frameworks containing unique stories, histories, and knowledges that can enrich our own. Thus each one of us has a moral responsibility to participate in bringing, especially submerged subaltern knowledge into light of day. Perhaps the following story can help us envision our moral responsibility in doing this.

When I was a child my grandmother used to tell me the story of a rabbit. "Once upon a time," she would say, "There was a man who went hunting in the forest. He trapped a rabbit. It was beautiful and he decided that he would bring it home and keep it caged as a pet. The man entrusted the care of the rabbit to his young daughter. Day in day out when the daughter would go to feed the rabbit, the rabbit would cry uncontrollably. One day she asked the rabbit, "Rabbit, every time I bring you food, you cry. What is wrong?" The rabbit replied that it misses the wild where other rabbits live. This made the daughter sad. She told the story to her father and prevailed on her father to let the rabbit go. One morning she came to the rabbit and said, "I have good news for you. You are free to go." She proceeded to open the cage and pronounced, "You are free, go!" When the rabbit tried to walk out it realized that its legs were heavy. It could not run as it used to. The rabbit had been caged for so long that it had lost the capacity to run. Every day since then the girl would come and tell the rabbit, "You are free, go." But the rabbit could not. The girl realized that she had a moral and ethical obligation to train the rabbit how to run again. She realized that the rabbit's lost capacity to run was her fault as well as her father's. Father and daughter took turns to play and run short distances with the rabbit. These short distances increased in length over time. One day as the girl ran, the rabbit out-ran her and disappeared into the wild." My grandmother would then tuck me in to sleep with the words, "my son, you are free to go — to grow into whomever you want to become and I am here to make sure that this happens."

Like in the above rabbit story, the legacy of imperial power over people — particularly the power over the mind (a people's knowledge system) can last for a long time.[76] Just like the daughter and her father we must all come to a realization of our complicity in the lack of or limited knowledge production, distribution, and consumption in the Majority World and take our responsibility to change this situation. We must all take on the burden of liberating others as our moral and ethical responsibility. We must tell the Majority World scholars that they are free to write, publish, and distribute their ideas and that we are here to make sure it happens. In circumstances where they can't take control of these processes we must start running short distances with them (read make steps towards their academic achievement and recognition in academia). And we ought to do this until they can run without our help.

If each one of us has a moral and ethical responsibility to the Majority World Other, what are the steps that we need to take to fulfil our role? What is the bridge between theory and praxes? The answer to these questions can be illuminated by the philosophies of Emmanuel Levinas and Paul Ricoeur.

---

[76]. This argument has eloquently been stated by Joy DeGruy in her book, *Post Traumatic Slave Syndrome: America's Legacy of Enduring Injury and Healing* (Portland, OR: Joy DeGruy Publications, Inc., 2005).

C. From Theory to Praxes: Levinas' Hermeneutics of "The Face" and Ricoeur's philosophy of "Oneself as Another"

In his philosophical formulations Emmanuel Levinas calls for the need to encounter the "face" of the Other." By encountering the "face" Levinas means encountering the Other not in terms of theoretical and empirical knowledge, but in terms of experiential knowledge — of meeting the other as a human being and understanding the sociopolitical and economic conditions that have formed who they are. When you encounter the "face," in this reality, Levinas argues that the "face" joins itself to you, not in the manner of superiority/inferiority category, but in the manner of equals — equals as fellow human beings. In this case the "destitution" and the "poverty" of the "face" which may seem to give you an advantageous status over the "face" is rather a call to responsibility, to service of the Other in order to create the united humanity, which according to Levinas must be a fraternal community.[77] If fraternity is a word that can define who we are as human beings, it goes without saying, therefore, that to erase, marginalize, or do violence against any group of human beings (in our case, marginalization of Majority World Knowledge), is an affront to human fraternity where no one comes out the winner.

Paul Ricoeur on his part makes an argument that humanity of oneself is constitutive of humanity of the Other to the extent that you cannot talk of oneself without talking of the other. Thus for him, the "selfhood of oneself implies otherness to such an intimate degree that one cannot be

---

77. Emmanuel Levinas, *Totality and Infinity: An Essay on Exteriority*, trans. Alphonso Lingis (Pittsburgh, PA: Duquesne University Press, 1969), 212–214.

thought of without the other."[78] In making this assertion, Ricoeur mediates between the Cartesian "I" consciousness as the absolute ground in abstraction with its relatedness (*cogito*) and the other extreme represented by Nietzsche, which is the idea that the "I" or selfhood is simply a rhetorical construct.[79] In between these two Ricoeur charts a third way, which is that to understand oneself, one is required to go through a rhetorical analyses of that "self." These analyses are provided through the linguistically mediated channels that require and invoke the "Other." In effect therefore, Ricoeur suggests that the definition of selfhood as an identity matters only because of the definition of the Other as an identity that stands to define the self.[80] In other words we exist as human beings in an ontological relationship with others. Thus the otherness of the Other does not belong to the outside of the language of self-definition. The Other is constitutive of the Self and that one is one's own body of flesh but a body only because it is defined by the presence of other bodies.[81] Thus Ricoeur's philosophy underscores the principle that our lives are intrinsically tied to other human beings in ways that we cannot entangle. We are each other and in each other. Understanding this principle can have far-reaching consequences on how we relate and treat each other. It would call us to the principle of collective perceptions on all realms of life. In this way it would help us conceive a world where the suffering of one becomes the suffering of all. And conversely one's well-being is constitutive of the well-being of all. In terms

---

78. Paul Ricoeur, *Oneself as Another*, trans. Kathleen Blamey (Chicago, IL: The University of Chicago Press, 1992), 3.

79. Ibid., 11–16.

80. Ibid., 138–139.

81. Ibid., 317.

of knowledge activism this means that a sustained effort to marginalize certain epistemological knowledge frameworks is in effect marginalizing one's own knowledge.

It is not too hard to illustrate the principles that Levinas and Ricoeur enunciate. In the summer of 2015, I was preparing to take a trip to from the US to Kenya, my country of birth. Money was tight and so before I left I planned my expenditures to the last penny. Everything went as planned until the last two days before I was to return to the US. On my second last day, I visited a high school friend. As he introduced me to his family, I noticed one child who had what looked like a sceptic wound. It looked horrible. I told my friend that his child should be taken to the hospital immediately. He answered that he had no money to pay the hospital bills. I could not look at that wound twice. I stepped out and called a friend in the US to loan and send me some money urgently. At this point my fiscal discipline did not matter anymore — a life of a child was on the line and that is what mattered to me. At that point I had come in an encounter with the "face" that Levinas talks about. In the child's wound and my friend's helplessness, I saw myself as a human being intrinsically bound to them in this need in the sense of Ricoeur's explanation. As Levinas says when you encounter the face, the face captures you, it arrests you into an interlocked gaze that you cannot simply entangle yourself and walk away. I could choose to ignore what I saw and concentrate on my plans to get back to the US. But I could only do that at the expense of my humanity. The "face" became a part of me, resisting my power to walk away. And it is this *apartness* that constitutes humanity.[82]

In relation to the above one can argue that the status of Majority World scholarship is in a sorry state. It requires

---

82. Levinas, *Totality and Infinity*, 214.

us to gaze at the "face" and take account of the "sick" state this scholarship is in. A few examples would suffice here to explain the sorry state. African scholarly publication represents only 2% of the world's academic publications.[83] Similarly Africa's share of global research output amounted to only 0.72% of the global research production in 2012.[84] The implication of this low rate of African scholarly output is that very few doctoral projects completed by Africans get to see the light of day as books. Because of the many impediments that make it impossible for Majority World scholars to write, publish, and distribute knowledge, the world runs only on Euro-American knowledge production machineries. The situation is comparable to a four-wheeled car that is running on only two wheels. It is because of this sickening status that we call the world to a moral responsibility to envision humanity by taking a gaze at the "face" of the Other and be interlocked with this gaze until it becomes a part of all of us.

In order to embrace the hermeneutics of the "face" one needs to encounter the "face." This "face" can be encountered in the work of generations of decolonial scholars who have privileged localized stories in specific communities in order to bring out the "destitution" and the "poverty" of the "face" and hence call humanity to social responsibility. Let me use the work of Walter D. Mignolo to illustrate this point. Mignolo traces the history, development, and legacy of coloniality, from the 1500s to the 2000s especially in Latin America. He argues that coloniality has bequeathed

---

83. Dan Ngabonziza and Jean de la Croix Tabaro, "Prof Romain Murenzi Reveals Africa's Academic Weakness," accessed 21 October 2015, http://ktpress.rw/prof-romain-murenzi-reveals-africas-academic-weakness-3442.

84. Mignonne Breier, "Africa: How Africa Is Tackling 'Next Generation' Fears in Academia," October 28, 2015, accessed November 2, 2015, http://allafrica.com/stories/201510301485.html?aa_source=nwsltr-education-en.

a Eurocentric knowledge system to modernity. This Eurocentric epistemological system has claimed the status of being "the" knowledge and in the process marginalized non-European knowledge epistemologies. In order to address this problem, Mignolo proposes an understanding and reorientation of the world through three concepts: Rewesternization (reconceiving of the Western world that values partnerships), Dewesterninization (re-conceiving a world that does not take Western epistemologies as the norm for understanding the rest of the world), and Decoloniality (divesting colonial power). According to Mignolo this reconceptualization of the world would inevitably usher in an explosion of knowledge narratives rather than "the" Eurocentric monolithic knowledge narrative.[85] According to Mignolo rewesternization is cognizant of the reality that gaining power can no longer use the route of imperial imposition. It rather would have to be enacted through diplomatic conversations that convolute and blur the superiority/inferiority binary identities. Imperial powers (including knowledge epistemological frameworks) would only gain status by disavowing the same. This creates a situation where the marginalized are brought to the negotiating table not in a weaker status, but as a partner for the common good.[86]

Dewesternization, a process started in Asian countries, is a protest against Western epistemological classifications of people according to color (White, Yellow, Black). The protest is not an effort to supplant Western epistemology, but one that affirms non-Western epistemological frameworks as being just as valid as Western ones. The end game is to impute dignity and honor to other ways of knowledge

---

85. Mignolo, *The Darker Side of Western Modernity*, 21.
86. Ibid., 35–44.

alongside Western knowledge.[87] And finally Mignolo argues for what he calls the "decolonial option." This is a process where the marginalized knowledges assert their status by delinking themselves from the Eurocentric epistemic systems. For Mignolo this is not to assert that other knowledges are better than Western epistemologies, but to suggest other options of epistemological frameworks that rapture the Eurocentric claim of owning "the" knowledge. This project is active among marginalized scholars and knowledge activists who question the status and politics of knowledge production, distribution, and consumption.[88] By doing this, these scholars and activists strip Western epistemological frameworks of the claim that it is "the" knowledge, "the" guardian of all knowing, and "the" guiding light of all world knowledges.[89]

According to Mignolo the above three processes are self-generative and self-propagating to the extent that the West can do nothing to stop them. The question that Mignolo does not address is what it would take for this to happen. Moreover, although what Mignolo states is not outside the realm of possibility, the over-confidence can easily blunt the overarching imperial power that has a very firm control on the Majority World and perhaps will for a long time to come. Additionally, although Mignolo is quick to point out that decolonial option is not meant to generate an epistemological system that supplants Western systems, he leaves the possibility to imagine rivalry binary distinctions between marginal knowledges and Eurocentric epistemological knowledge. As Cecilia Tossounian suggests, such duality shrinks the dialogue space between Western schol-

---

87. Ibid., 44–52.
88. Ibid., 52–62.
89. Ibid., 82.

ars and marginal world scholars.[90] What I advocate rather is for both Majority World and Euro-American scholars to encounter the "face," that is, to come to a social awareness of the negative effects of epistemological racism — to know that it hurts all of us. Hopefully this understanding will soften our hearts and change our praxes. We need to effect changes in our hearts rather than leave them to utopian natural causalities as Mignolo would suggest. Anzaldúa has a point when she states that no change happens in the real world unless it has happened first in our minds and hearts.[91]

In the following section we suggest that knowledge epistemological frameworks, in terms of who is marginalized, lend themselves to fluid identities and fluid deployments that leave no room for the viability and importance of exclusive knowledge identity.

---

90. Cecilia Tossounian, Review of Walter Mignolo, Bulletin of Latin American Research, JS*LAS* 33:3 (2014): 370–372.

91. Cf., Anzaldúa, *Borderlands/La Frontera*, 109.

III. RECASTING SUBALTERNITY, MARGINALITY AND PRIVILEGE AS FLUID IDENTITIES

R.S. Wafula

There is so much fluidity between who is/is not marginalized in terms of knowledge processes that in the end no one benefits from knowledge(s) marginalization. In this section I discuss this under three subheadings.

A. Fluid Subalternity, Marginality, and Privilege Between Euro-American Contexts and Majority World Contexts

The title of one of Hamid Dabashi's books is *Can Non-Europeans Think?* This book is written in the context of a diatribe between European and non-European philosophers. Dabashi answers his question in the affirmative making a case that thinking is imbedded in the very nature of human life.[92] However, Dabashi's book raises the larger question of *knowability*. Who can know? How can one know? The guide to the answer to these questions requires us to rumi-

---

92. Hamid Dabashi, *Can Non-Europeans Think?* (London: Zed Boks, 2015), 1–43.

nate on another set of questions, which are: who is on the margins? Who is not? Is knowledge a reserve of one group over the other? The questions lead us to the idea that the privilege to know casting one as the master of knowledge and the others as subalterns is fluid. This fluidity disavows superiority and calls for an epistemological shift that liberalizes the processes of knowledge production, distribution, and consumption, for the common good.

Dabashi argues that when he wrote an essay on Al Jazeera website with the same title as his book, *Can Non-Europeans Think?* he was shedding light on the work of non-European thinkers. However, two European philosophers, Santiago Zabala and Slavoj Žižek, operating under the assumption that thinking (philosophy) is a European reserve, thought that Dabashi was writing about them and their philosophy. Hence they wrote response essays to defend their turf (philosophy) against intruders (non-European philosophers). By doing this Dabashi argues that the European thinkers took it that the world rotates around them — and that nothing philosophical can be done outside their epistemological framework. But in sustaining this framework, these European philosophers missed the train of so much philosophy being done outside their frameworks. According to Dabashi they had no clue about his work or that of any non-European thinker beyond their world. They had no reason or interest to learn anything outside of themselves since philosophy is European philosophy. And if there is anything non-European that sounds philosophical it must be coopted back into European philosophy where it belongs.[93]

In other words, one can make an argument that by sustaining an "all knowing" attitude, Eurocentric epistemol-

---

93. Ibid., 3–5.

ogy becomes unknowledgeable about the epistemological developments in other parts of the world. Thus, and ironically, their knowability claims (superiority) generates their unknowability status (inferiority). Let me illustrate this oscillation and fluidity between knowledge, power, and privilege with a reference to the deployment of Kenyan people — most of them against their will — to fight for the British colonial imperialists in both World War I and II. Although these Kenyan people were helpless victims fighting in wars they did not understand, the wars gave them a totally new perspective on their colonizers. While fighting alongside Europeans, they witnessed casualties among both the Kenyan and British (and other European) soldiers. They realized that European soldiers were just as vulnerable in war as Kenyan people. Bildad Kaggia, one of the Kenyan soldiers, reflects on this experience. He states that before the war, many of them were led to believe that Europeans were superior. But after participating in the war and seeing Europeans get killed in war the African soldiers came to a conclusion that "the European is just like us." He can get killed too.[94]

While the Africans were gaining new insights about gun warfare and the vulnerabilities of the combatants, the British colonizers did not think that these "backward uneducated" Kenyans would learn anything beyond firing the guns as commanded by British army commanders. The British took it that knowledge and learning is a reserve for Europeans and not Africans. But in their superiority claim of knowledge, they ironically became the unknowledgeable ones. The Kenyan soldiers had the capacity to learn

---

94. Eric Onstad, "WWII Lives on Among African Veterans Who Returned Home as Freedom Fighters," *Los Angeles Times*, n.p., November 5, 1989, accessed April 1, 2016, http://articles.latimes.com/1989-11-05/news/mn-1369_1_world-war-ii.

beyond the artificial colonial delimitations. The Kenyans had learned a lot about the art of warfare, the strategies of resistance, and the need to fight for freedom. They had also learned a lot about British weaknesses. When they returned to Kenya, they employed their new skills, often snatching British colonialist weapons, to fight for Kenya's freedom. This newfound military knowledge became the bedrock for the formation of the Mau Mau resistance movement in Kenya. The British were caught off-guard about the newfound Kenyan knowledge and in the long run their colonial power over Kenya started becoming a costly affair. Knowledge, power, and control had become so fluid that it blurred the boundaries between British superiority and Kenyans' inferiority to the extent that the British colonialists had to concede defeat for the control of the Kenyan colony.

The same can be said of Majority World intellectuals. Starting in the 1960s to date there has been a successive wave of Africans going to Euro-American centers of education. These scholars learn Euro-American epistemological systems. In time they begin understanding the fallacy of these epistemological systems. These scholars, upon returning home (and those who remain in the Euro-American centers of academia) use their newfound knowledge to resist Eurocentric epistemological frameworks. Thus increasingly the postcolonial condition of marginalization generates new Majority World epistemological thinking that seeks to showcase Majority World scholarship that leaves no room for monolithic Eurocentric views of knowledge. And as Dabashi says unless the Eurocentric epistemological framework is dismantled, Euro-American scholars (and those who operate within their framework) will miss out on so much of the knowledge that is unfolding in Majority World contexts.[95] Like the two European scholars in Dabashi's story, or British colonialists in the Kenyan case cited above, the Euro-American scholars would become surprised that non-Europeans can also think, even when that surprise should be unfounded. After all, most of these "thinking" non–Euro-Americans were trained by Euro-American scholars in the Euro-American academy centers in the first place.

For this reason, Dabashi advocates for a situation where Eurocentric epistemological frameworks would dismount the Kantian binary discourse where the European is the knowing subject and the Other as the knowable subject. According to him this European knowing subject was a European construct that does not exist. Thus, "We must dismantle the fact that we are each other's figment of imagination."[96] We must dislodge the binary link of the knowing subject and the knowable object and rather establish an epistemological framework of learning about each other with each other.[97] In this case just like Majority World thinkers (scholars) understand European knowledge by reading and engaging European scholarship, Euro-American scholars need to make deliberate concerted efforts to learn new ideas from the Majority World scholars. For example, rather than google "Africa" or read information written by Euro-American scholars on Africa, Euro-American scholars will understand Africa better if they read and engage African scholars and scholarship. Rather than having a world that subscribes to "the" knowledge (Eurocentric epistemology) we need to create a world that subscribes to all knowledges. In this epistemological framework there is no room

---

95. Ibid., 6.
96. Ibid., 23.
97. Ibid., 16, 24.

for "the" philosophy (meaning European philosophy) as opposed to ethno-philosophy (meaning philosophy of other identities). Rather the academic world should have plenty of room for all philosophies: European philosophy, African philosophy, Latin American philosophy, Asian philosophy, and so forth. In this way knowledge becomes liberalized around localized identities and the acknowledgement that to know (as in all knowledge) requires a deliberate effort to get out of one's framework and learn from the Other. It also requires one to accept that what one knows is limited to one's provincialized setting and that outside that setting is something that is unknown. In order to know the unknown outside one's limits, one needs, what Dabashi calls, a democratic field where the subject of knowledge knows that what they know is only one among many other knowledges.[98]

If this acknowledgement can be made, it would totally reshape the present binary status of epistemological knowledge frameworks pitting Eurocentric epistemologies against the Majority World epistemologies. It can help policy makers to start effecting changes in the education curriculums, usage of textbooks, scholarly citations, professional academic praxes, and the whole machinery of knowledge production, distribution, and consumption. Let me for a moment reflect on these items and the present imbalance they create and how this imbalance depicts the fluidity of knowing/not knowing between the West and the Majority World. Most of Euro-American high school geography and history is very Eurocentric and does not expose their students in a significant way to the history and geography of other parts of the world. As a result, an average American high school student can hardly tell,

---

98. Ibid., 37.

for example, where Angola, Kenya, or Botswana is on the African map, or what goes on in these countries.[99] On the contrary, Majority World curriculums have extensive history and geography lessons of not only Majority World places but also on Euro-American geopolitics spheres. For example, an average Kenyan high school student can easily name all of the fifty US states and almost any aspect of the history, geography and the politics of the US. In other words, while the Euro-American epistemic knowledge systems claim centrality and supremacy of "all knowledge," they underprepare their citizens to understand the world around them, leaving them increasingly on the fringes of knowledge about the world beyond their own countries. On the other hand, their counterparts in the Majority World increasingly gain knowledge about Euro-American spaces, becoming informed and knowledgeable even when the Eurocentric epistemic narratives describe them otherwise.

This situation is worsened by the lack of the use of Majority World scholarship in Euro-American schools and colleges.[100] Of course all this may have to do with the imperial idea that there is nothing that can be learned from outside of these imperial centers of knowledge. Thus the majority of those who go through Euro-American colleges do not benefit from the knowledge production of Africans, Latin Americans, Asians and any other Majority World scholarship. In their consumption of only Western epistemic knowledge, they become unknowledgeable about

---

99. I am not just making this up. Every semester I begin classes by telling my American liberal arts college students that I am originally from Kenya. I then ask then to pinpoint Kenya on the African continental map. Most of the students get it wrong.

100. Through my graduate years of school both in Scotland (a year) and the US (about ten years) there was scanty bibliographic use of Majority World scholarship.

the rest of the knowledge production in the world. On the contrary, the Majority World colleges expose students to world-wide literature, philosophy, history, geography and so forth. I remember in my high school the literature syllabus included items such as Charles Dickens's *Oliver Twist*, Henrik Ibsen's *An Enemy of the People*, V.S. Naipaul's *A House for Mr. Biswas*, Ivan Turgenev's *Fathers and Sons*, Arthur Miller's *The Death of a Salesman*, and George Orwell's *Animal Farm*, among others. These stories exposed us to the Euro-American and outside literary world, besides African literature. In a sense our intellectual growth gave us world-wide epistemological perspective. Hence one cannot describe a Majority World educated person as being on the margins of knowledge acquisition. On the contrary it is the Euro-American educated person who occupies the marginal status in terms of knowledge acquisition.

In the academic community, there is a dearth of citation of Majority World scholarship by Euro-American scholars, yet this is the only system that propels and controls the knowability of the "who is who" and "what is what" in any given academic field. The more one is cited, the more one becomes a household name and the more the knowledge they produce gets to be widely circulated around the world. Since Eurocentric epistemological framework hardly recognizes Majority World scholarship, much of this knowledge and those who produce it in Majority World contexts are sidelined in the fields within which they write. Reflecting on this problem, Madipoane Masenya (Ngwan'a Mphahlele) states:

> Research has revealed that Western scholars basically do not refer or quote non-Western (read: African) canons. The preceding revelation was confirmed by my review of the twentieth anniversary edition of Women's Bible Commentary.

I cited the example of HB womanist scholar, Renita Weems, whose framework is outside of mainstream feminist biblical hermeneutics. Most of the authors, who encaged some of the prophetic books, highlighted the problematic metaphor of Yahweh as a faithful Husband and Israel as a disobedient wife. They revealed the effects which such a metaphor had and continue to have on the lives of flesh and blood women. What I found revealing is that despite the fact that Weems was one of the earlier women scholars who engaged such metaphors, only one author, who is probably of African descent referred to Weems' work.[101]

Thus Masenya highlights a problem that is so pervasive in academia that even when Euro-American scholars are aware of the works of their Majority World peers, they consciously choose not to cite them into their work. What Masenya points out can be illustrated with the buzz about the origin of a postcolonial theory. In Western academia, this origin is credited to the hollowed-trinitarian reference to Edward Said, Gayatri Chakravorty Spivak, and Homi Bhabha. You would imagine that such scholarship would have begun their citations with the works of Albert Memmi, Frantz Fanon, Ngũgĩ Wa Thiong'o, and Mosala Itumeleng, among others. Why would postcolonial scholars ignore the latter? One of the fundamental reasons is that Said, Spivak, and Bhabha write in highly theoretical and abstract frameworks that are characteristic of Western epistemological writings. In so doing they fail to connect their theories to tangible and practical lived experiences of communities for which they purport to represent. They write to hold conversations with a purely academic audi-

---

[101]. Madipoane Masenya (Ngwan'a Mphahlele), "For Ever Trapped? An African Voice on Insider/Outsider Dynamics Within South African Old Testament Gender-Sensitive Frameworks," *OTSSA* 27:1 (2014): 189–204.

ence and not with communities of marginalized peoples.[102] Thus these scholars are allies with Euro-American scholars/scholarship. Because of this Euro-American scholarship finds it easy to celebrate and cite them. In this zeal Western academia falsely imputes upon the three the honor of fathering/mothering postcolonial theorization above other scholars who do not theorize in Western epistemological formulations. I would like to posit that another reason has to do racial stratification of peoples that puts the white person at the top of the ladder, the brown colors in the middle spaces, and the black-colored people at the very bottom. In this sense Said, Spivak, and Bhabha who theorize about the Middle Eastern/Indian natives, occupy the next best racial group after the whites. But since Memmi, Fanon, Wa Thiong'o, and Mosala theorize about African and black people, their work has no academic sympathy among the Eurocentric academic cycles. The three theorize about a people that are not supposed to be 'bearers of knowledge.' They are objects to be studied and not subjects of study or subjects who can study/research. Thus the problem against citing African scholars and scholarship is not only about the negated racial identity of the scholar but also about the racialized identity of the body of scholarship. In the scheme of Eurocentric epistemological frameworks postcolonialism, which is meant to frame discourses of resistance against colonial/imperial narratives, cannot originate among the marginalized colonized subjects. It has to be coopted into Western epistemological discourses.

However, by co-opting postcolonialism Euro-American epistemological frameworks detach theory from praxes emptying words, as Freire states, of their concreteness and

---

102. See R.S. Wafula, *Biblical Representations of Moab: A Kenyan Postcolonial Reading* (New York, NY: Peter Lang, 2014), 39–50.

making them hollow, empty and alienating verbosity.[103] This is particularly accented in Eurocentric argument that when we talk about postcolonialism, we should not privilege the contemporary nineteenth century colonial period — that we should also, in equal measure, talk about all imperial contexts/periods going back to ancient empires. Although this line of argument makes perfect sense, it has given Euro-American biblical scholars a comfortable zone — a retreat center where they can theoretically talk about empire in ancient imperial contexts and texts and leave the conversation just there — in the past where it belongs with no praxiological implications to the contemporary communities.[104] Thus these Euro-American scholars, while disavowing privileging one context (contemporary colonial contexts) over another (ancient ones), end up doing exactly what they disavow by privileging ancient contexts over contemporary contexts. In so doing they build a wall that makes them unwilling and unable to accept that Majority World scholars have anything important to say about the postcolonial condition — a condition that to Majority World scholars and people in general is not a historical discourse, but something written and being written everyday on their bodies and affecting their everyday lives.[105] This situation makes the Euro-American scholars miss out on the intelligence and work of others, a situation that limits their knowledge in the midst of much Eurocentric knowledge production. In the process these Eurocentric scholars end

---

103. Freire, *Pedagogy of the Oppressed*, 71.

104. Many of the essays in the collection *A Postcolonial Commentary on the New Testament Writings* edited by Fernando F. Segovia and R.S. Sugirtharajah lends themselves to this charge.

105. I am using the designation 'Euro-American" scholars in some limited sense since there is a significant number of Euro-American scholars who are willing to listen and engage the voices of the victims of imperial power.

up marginalizing their very intelligentsia through claims to know all that there is to know. While this Eurocentric self-marginalization is taking place, Majority World scholars are privileged not only by knowing their own knowledge production, but also by consuming Euro-American scholarship hence getting the best of both knowledge–epistemological worlds.

One can also talk of inter-cultural interactions in the context of crossing borders. Most of the mass movement of people from Euro-American geopolitical spaces to Majority World contexts is a touristic (ad)venture with people on holiday, business trips, or government representatives out to help "helpless" Majority World people. By and large journeys are not undertaken with the intent of learning, of education, of seeking to know from the Majority World people. If knowledge is the reason, the journey is about confirming what they (Euro-American sojourners) already know. It is about collecting data to support an already framed hypothesis about the Majority World people. Thus Euro-American learning is not a question of learning from the Majority World people. It is rather one of learning about Majority World peoples using already established Euro-American epistemological frameworks. On the other hand, the human traffic from Majority World to Euro-American contexts consists mostly of people who are going there for graduate school education. Learning is the primary reason for these journeys. Most of the Majority World scholars return to their countries, not only armed with the education they received but also with box-loads of Euro-American books they would have acquired in the course of their studies. The end result is that a Majority World scholar, though occupying the spaces of marginality in Euro-American epistemological imaginations, comes out as a finished product — a well-rounded, educated individual. On the other hand, a Euro-American scholar, though having all the resources to become knowledgeable, ends up being a product of limited knowledge — a captive victim of the Eurocentric epistemological limited knowledge framework. Marginality in terms of academic power envisioned this way becomes a fluid concept where the privileged becomes the underprivileged and the other way round.

In order to address this oscillating and endless problem, the two academic worlds (the Euro-American and Majority World) need to meet on a common level ground that is not framed in terms of competing superiority/inferiority terms, but on equal terms that enrich the world's knowledge circulation.

B. Fluid Subalternity, Marginality, and Privilege Between Diaspora Majority World Scholars and 'On-the-Continent' Majority World Scholars

One of the most formidable weapons of colonization was a concept called "divide and rule" or "divide and conquer." Peres Owino has written and directed a movie documentary called *Africans and African Americans: Silent Sibling Rivalry*. The documentary depicts the differences between two otherwise loving brothers born in "the land of warm waters (Africa)." Suddenly one brother is torn from the other (by the cruelty of European slave trade) never to be seen again. The one brother waits at the waters' edge all his life for his brother to come back. When he grows old and is about to die, he charges his son to do the same. This goes on for generations until several hundred years later, in the land of cold waters (America), the daughters of the two brothers meet. But when this happens they just walk past each other, one never noticing the other. How did these descendants of two loving brothers become so isolated? The journey to the answer begins with Africans and African-Americans recounting personal, hurtful experiences with each other."[106]

Part of the answer to the question lies in the colonizer's narrative that the Africans on the continent bear the sole responsibility for slave trade. They are the ones who sold their fellow Africans. Since this is the narrative that the African Americans receive they naturally develop hatred against their fellow kin on the continent. The documentary goes on to also showcase the often false impression among African Americans that the Africans on the continent live a much better life (since they do not have to deal with everyday racism and imperialism) than the African Americans. However, the reality that the documentary portrays is different; which is that though divided geopolitically and historically, all Africans on either divide are still victims of the same imperial power. Thus rather than continue embracing the dialect of binary construction, the documentary urges for unity between Africans on the continent and Africans in the diaspora and concerted efforts among these groups to eliminate colonial power over both of them.

In more recent times, the African divide is replaying itself out again in scholarship circles. A research conducted by Paul Tiyambe Zeleza for the Carnegie Corporation of New York in 2011 and 2012 shows that some African scholars on the continent resent African scholars in the diaspora (in Euro-American geopolitical spaces).[107] According to Zeleza,

---

106. Peres Owino, "Bound: Africans vs. African Americans," Nyarnam Productions, 2014, accessed January 18, 2016, https://itunes.apple.com/us/movie/bound-africans-vs-african/id989662587.

107. The reference to the African diaspora here does not refer to African Americans (descendants of slavery) but to more recent African immigrants.

part of the resentment stems from the perspective that African diaspora scholars have abandoned their African continent to serve colonial interests (academia) and hence are tools of colonial epistemologies, continuing the marginalization of their fellow African scholars on the continent through their writings and stories about Africa. Additionally the scholars on the continent often accuse diaspora scholars of passing themselves as representatives of Africa to the outside world, negating and sidelining the "true" representatives who are the scholars on the continent.[108]

Some of these accusations are not entirely without merit. Gerald West points this out in his discussion of the work of Edward Said, Homi Bhabha, Gayatri Chakravorty Spivak, and R.S. Sugirtharajah; whereas he notes their significant contributions, he is apprehensive about their scholarly agendas. He argues that their hermeneutical lenses are influenced by Western knowledge epistemological frameworks to the extent that their scholarship is devoid of liberationist perspectives, which is a fundamental characteristic of Majority World scholarship. However, Said, Bhabha, and Spivak are not representative of a vast majority of diasporic scholars. As a result, a significant number of us would dispute West's argument if in fact it veers towards generalizations of these scholars and their scholarship. Many Majority World scholars remain in the Euro-American academic centers for reasons beyond their control. Most of them, as stated elsewhere in this project, are heavily invested in the academic concerns of their fellow Majority World scholars and contexts. A number of them

---

108. Paul Tiyambe Zeleza, "Engagements between African Diaspora Academics in the US and Canada and African Institutions of Higher Education: Perspectives from North America and Africa," (Nov. 2008): 1–37, accessed March 30, 2016, http://www.iie.org/~/media/Files/Programs/Carnegie-African-Diaspora-Fellows-Program/Carnegie-Engage.

like George Sefa Dei and myself (among others), although located in Canada and the United States, respectively, consciously make Africa the subject of their scholarship. One other challenge that can be brought to bear on West's argument is that location alone is not a determinant of a scholar's commitments and passion. West assumes that the center of Eurocentric knowledge epistemologies is Europe and the US — that African scholars are immune from Eurocentric knowledge epistemologies. On the contrary, most African centers of education are replicas of Euro-centric epistemologies. In relation to just the curriculum Patrick Mbataru asks; "Whose content is it? Is what we are teaching at the university ours [African]?"[109] Of course the answers to Mbataru's questions is in the negative. The reality, as Mbataru continues, is that "we inherited the university system lock, stock and barrel from those who colonized us."[110] What this means is that even African scholars who are on the continent are in some ways immersed in the colonial knowledge systems. Consciously or unconsciously they participate in some ways to perpetuate these systems. As a result, location of a scholar alone cannot be the determinant of a scholar's commitment to social justice and emancipation of African scholarship. The fight for social justice is a deliberate choice that some make while others don't regardless of their social location.

However, granted that some Majority World scholars, as West points out, get coopted in Western epistemologies, one can ask, how can a Majority World scholar fail to uphold the sensitivities of engaged scholarship in their theorizing?

---

109. Patrick Mbataru, "Kenyan Universities Have Lost the Edge," *Standard*, September 20, 2016, accessed September 20, 2016, http://www.standardmedia.co.ke/article/2000216751/kenyan-universities-have-lost-the-edge.

110. Ibid.

Smith answers this question. She argues that academic writing by its very nature is a process that involves selecting, arranging, and presenting knowledge in terms of what matters to the author and their targeted audience. Some Majority World scholars write primarily for a Euro-American audience (and also generally to the academic audience); hence they inevitably privilege certain ways of storytelling to appeal to their target audience. Since they write for a Eurocentric academic audience, Smith argues that whenever they write about themselves or their own peoples, they write with an outsider view, thus sustaining the Euro-American epistemological frameworks that hold the Other as unimportant.[111] In comparison to Euro-American ways of writing engaged scholars on the other hand write from the inside — as members of the community. These scholars do not just write about abstract academic discourses in their fields. They rather write out of the wealth of lived experiences of colonization and oppression in order to provide a road map for liberation.[112] Thus scholarship has to do with deliberate perspectives to serve intended interests rather than even one's location. Some scholars, whether located in Euro-American or in Majority World academic centers, choose to locate themselves within the Euro-centric knowledge epistemologies while others located on either of these two centers of academia choose to work within the realm of social justice focusing on the welfare of all, and particularly the marginalized. As Smith puts it, it a choice between being an unengaged (Eurocentric) and engaged scholar.

---

111. Smith, *Decolonizing Methodologies*, 37.

112. Gerald West, "Doing Postcolonial Biblical Interpretation @Home: Ten of (South) African Ambivalence," *Neotestamentica* 42.1 (2008): 147–164.

The diaspora and "on-the-continent" scholars' binary divide is not unique to the African continent. The phenomenon bedevils Latin American scholars as well.[113] According to Ramón Grosfoguel one of the main reasons for the split for them is the feeling that some Latin American scholars were, what Grosfoguel calls, *Latinamericanists* who reproduced a Euro-American epistemic schema in their discourses about South American peoples. In the American universities' area studies departments these scholars became the experts (knowing subject) of the South American people (objects to be known). In so doing they played into the Euro-American epistemic knowledge system of the Westerner as the master of all knowledge denying the South American-located Latina scholars (subjects) space to represent themselves. For Grosfoguel, therefore, the decolonial option should encompass the voices of the geopolitical scholars located in the so-called Third World places not in the framework of identity politics, but in the notion that epistemological frameworks are multiple and hold equal status.[114]

Although West and Grosfoguel are very specific about the diasporic scholars they reference, the flavor of their essays open up a can of worms that can be exploited, stereotypically, to exacerbate the hostilities between Majority World scholars residing in Euro-American contexts as opposed

---

113. Other scholars who argue for the recognition of marginalized epistemologies include: Gloria Anzaldúa, *Borderlands/La Frontera* (San Francisco, CA: Spinsters, 1987), and Jose David Saldívar, *Trans-Americanity: Subaltern Modernities, Global Coloniality, and the Cultures of Greater Mexico (New Americanists)* (Durham, NC: Duke University Press, 2012).

114. Ramón Grosfoguel, "Decolonizing Post-Colonial Studies and Paradigms of Political Economy: Transmodernity, Decolonial Thinking, and Global Coloniality," *Transmodernity: JPPLHW 1:1* (2011): n.p. accessed April 2, 2016, http://dialogoglobal.com/texts/grosfoguel/Grosfoguel-Decolonizing-Pol-Econ-and-Postcolonial.pdf.

to those who reside and work in Majority World contexts. West's charge is particularly illustrative of this temptation. He states, "some of those who have moved to other sites of struggle in the center of empire should not elide those who remain @home and who get their hands dirty and dare to dream in actual postcolonial contexts, using whatever resources seem useful, including postcolonial discourse."[115] The question is, who determines those whose "hands are getting dirty"? Who decides which scholars are fighting for social justice for the welfare of marginalized Third World scholars? What is the criteria for this determination? According to West, location is determinant. It is only those who are resident on the African continent (in the case of West) who are pro-social justice for marginalized communities. This is a fallacy. As already argued body location does not automatically grant a scholar the social justice commitments. A scholar's commitment to the welfare of the marginalized is a choice that can be made by any scholar in any part of the world regardless of their social location. In this regard, one can even make a case that some of the passionate scholarship for justice is being produced by Majority World scholars in diaspora. Thus West's charge stereotypically misrepresents the Majority World diaspora scholars as those who do not "get their hands dirty." This can cause an unnecessary rift between Majority World scholars on the continent and those in the diaspora and lead them to easily succumb to the divide and rule tactics that can hamper unity among them and deny them a much higher collective bargaining power towards liberating themselves and others they represent from Euro-American epistemological knowledge frameworks.

---

115. West, "Doing Postcolonial Biblical Interpretation @Home," 164.

The good news, however, is that efforts (at least on the African continent) are being done to bridge the gap between scholars in the diaspora and scholars who reside and work on the continent. Reflecting on these efforts, Wachira Kigotho states the following concerning African scholars in the diaspora: "Whatever the various vagaries and fortunes that compelled its members to stay abroad — either as political or economic refugees, or as 'non-returnees' after further studies — the African academic diaspora seems united in its resolve to bridge the intellectual and economic gaps that afflict most universities."[116] So contrary to West's words that only the scholars on the continent are the ones who "get dirty," Majority World diaspora scholars gladly want to take their fair share of this dirtiness. Some of the efforts to get diaspora African scholars to "get dirty" are being championed, among others, by the Carnegie African Diaspora Fellowship Program, under the Carnegie Foundation of New York. Through this program African scholars in the US and Canada are reaching out for research collaborations with fellow African scholars on the African continent. The Foundation's African Program goal is stated as "to facilitate equitable, effective and mutually beneficial international higher education engagements between scholars in Africa and African Diaspora academics in Canada and the United States."[117] The plan is to solicit and engage African scholars in the diaspora to go back to African universities to help spur research and scholarship engagements with African scholars on the continent.

---

116. Wachira Kigotho, "Are African Universities Ready for Diaspora Academics?" *University World News*, April 2, 2016, accessed April 4, 2016, http://www.universityworldnews.com/article.php?story=20160401171348654.

117. *Vision*, Carnegie African Diaspora Fellowship Program, accessed April 5, 2016, http://www.iie.org/en/Programs/Carnegie-African-Diaspora-Fellows-Program/Vision.

However, the framework can easily lend itself to the false dichotomy of "African diaspora scholars "who know" versus African scholars on the continent "who don't know" and who needs to be brought up to speed with "Western knowledge" eliciting the memories of Eurocentric epistemological colonization. If the Carnegie Foundation does not consciously tame this notion, the program can easily be a one-way train as stated elsewhere in this book, going to Africa full of "knowledge goodies" in the name of diaspora scholars and returning to the US empty with no reciprocal exchange with African scholars on the continent. In order to destabilize this notion, Postcolonial Networks and Borderless Press as explained in this book are premised on the ideal that African scholars (and indeed the rest of the Majority World) are the masters of their knowledge. What the two organizations do therefore is not to "teach" those who don't know but to provide an avenue for the Majority World scholars to produce that knowledge and inject it into the currency of the world's knowledge economy. The aim is thus to advocate and facilitate the production of more Majority World scholarship rather than teach them what they need to know.

At Postcolonial Networks and Borderless Press, we operate with the understanding that colonial epistemologies marginalize other knowledges through a series of intentional projects that include representing a Euro-American epistemological framework as the standard and only way of knowing. Since Euro-American scholars "know" and Majority World scholars do not "know," the Euro-American scholar takes on the white man's burden of educating the unintelligent Majority World scholars. Through this process the Majority World knowledge is erased, de-faced and demeaned. As a result of this, Postcolonial Networks and

Borderless Press' decolonial project involves programs to re-humanize Majority World knowledge by allowing the scholars in these contexts to speak in their own voice and to give them a platform to be heard. As many of these voices become book projects and injected into academia, the world will get to know these contexts from their own "experts" hence correcting some of the false notions about the Majority World geopolitical locales current in Euro-American scholarship. Ours is a two-way train. We sent African scholars in the diaspora (together with our Euro-American friends) to Africa to initiate research collaborations, and writing and publishing workshops. When the train returns to the USA, oftentimes it returns with African scholars that come into some three-months writing residencies in the US. While here these scholars give back to the US university hosts through sharing their research, teaching, and writing. Then the train goes to cycle again in this endless give and take of epistemological enrichment.

Perhaps it is important for Majority World scholars either in diaspora or on the continents of their birth to know how Mignolo's idea of colonial "difference" (as argued elsewhere in this book) and Owino's documentary show that colonial frameworks do not treat colonial and postcolonial victims constructed as the "Other" any differently regardless of their geopolitical and social locations. In terms of mapping and constructing these victims, Euro-American epistemological frameworks circulate and migrate all around the world, following the "negro" wherever he/she is. Thus in the US where I teach, I am classified as an academician of color or of a minority status, alongside other "colors." Sometimes I get the rare privilege to overhear conversations such as, "black scholars are not hired because of their academic intelligence, but to meet the 'affirmative action' quotas of the college." As a result, in order for me to defend myself and articulate my postcoloniality my hands get "dirty" every day just as my fellow African scholars on the continent. In this regard I do not possess the status of power and privilege that my fellow African scholars on the continent would impute on me. I am rather an endangered small fish species swimming in a dangerous sea of Euro-American academic sharks.[118] Sometimes I wish I was teaching in Kenya or some African university rather than here in the US. Oftentimes I fantasize about things such as being respected for my work, being no affirmative action appointee, being addressed by my students and the community at large as "Daktari" (Doctor) and gaining the status that comes with that. In my fantasy I imagine how privileged my fellow African scholars on the continent are. But this fantasy and daydreaming lasts only until I visit, talk, and collaborate with fellow African scholars on the continent. Then I am rudely woken out of my slumber with the stark reality that even on the continent there is a fluidity of subalternity, marginality, and privilege that reigns supreme.

C. Fluid Subalternity, Marginality, and Privilege Among Majority World Scholars in the Majority World Geopolitical Settings

It seems that ethnic/tribal affiliations and all its negative manifestations follow Kenyans (and this applies to many

---

[118]. The reality I am articulating here is that Majority World Scholars who live in Euro-American contexts should know better than to surrender the struggle and fail to stand alongside their fellow scholars on the continents of marginality (as Smith and West lament). These scholars should know that however much they work for acceptability, the very best they would earn are tokens of endowed chairs to continue impersonating and (mis)representing their fellow colonized victims while supporting the Euro-American epistemological machinery of knowledge production, dissemination, and consumption.

other African contexts as well) everywhere and in everything. We breathe, talk, and live tribally. There would be nothing wrong in that had it not been that these existential praxes carry with them the baggage of privilege or lack of it. They determine who lives and who dies either in the physical sense of the word or in all of its metaphorical senses. As Koigi Wa Wamwere points out, negative ethnic identifications permeate and determine everything from politics, economics, and social life to employment opportunities in Majority World contexts. It gives enormous privilege to those who belong on the right side of tribal power and all things genocidal to those on the wrong side of this in power.[119] In this section I reflect only on ethnic identification as it relates to academic employment procedures in Kenya. One would imagine that a PhD being the highest academic award in any field should level the employment field for all who possess it. However, this is not the case in Kenya. It seems that in Kenya, employing the *Animal Farm* metaphor, some animals are more equal than others. According to the Chairperson of Kenya's National Cohesion and Integration Commission (NCIC), Francis Ole Kaparo, the academic and even administrative leadership of most Kenyan universities are dominated by people from one or two particular tribes at the expense of all the other forty two Kenyan tribes.[120] This reality becomes grim when one puts the figures into play. One local Kenyan newspaper (*The Standard*) reports:

---

[119]. Koigi Wa Wamwere, *Negative Ethnicity: From Bias to Genocide* (New York, NY: Seven Stories Press, 2003), 44–50.

[120]. Linah Benyawa, "Public Universities Promoting Tribalism in Kenya, NCIC Warns," *Standard*, August 8, 2015, accessed January 20, 2016, http://www.standardmedia.co.ke/article/2000172071/public-universities-promoting-tribalism-in-kenya-ncic-warns.

> An audit of public universities has revealed that the institutions have become incubators of ethnicity ... majority of staff either come from the same ethnic group as the Vice-Chancellor, the principal or the locality of the institution ... Out of the 14,996 workers in the institutions surveyed Kikuyu, Luhya, Kalenjin, Luo and Kisii dominate the institutions of higher learning. [of these the] Kikuyu are the majority at 4,133 (27.6 per cent), Luhya 2,544 (17.0 per cent), Kalenjin 2,133 (14.2), Luo 2,086 (13.9 per cent) and Kisii 1,253 (8.4 per cent) ... [The] five ethnic groups make up 81 per cent of the workforce in the institutions, leaving the remaining 37 tribes to share out the rest.[121]

What the above state of affairs means is that academic employment, assignments, and promotions are not dependent on a person's qualifications or service. They are rather based on tribal affiliation. Those who come from the "right" tribe (of those in power) would be automatically favored at all levels in academia over their peers who come from the "wrong" tribe. As a result, teaching and doing research in such environments requires a careful negotiation and balancing act for those who are from the "wrong" tribe. The research and work of those who belong to the "wrong" tribe is valued less than the work of those who belong to the "right" tribe. Those who belong to the "right" tribe, backed with a sense of entitlement, have a free rein in all matters. They would often access more privileges to research, travel grants to academic conferences, and gain scholarships for academic advancement than those who belong to the "wrong" tribe. In the end you find a situation that is no

---

121. Peter Opiyo, "Shock of Tribalism in Public Universities," *Standard*, March 7, 2012, accessed January 20 2016, http://www.standardmedia.co.ke/business/article/2000053553/shock-of-tribalism-in-public-universities.

different from the colonial difference that Mignolo refers to as discussed earlier in this book.

As a result of the above a significant number of Majority World scholars decide to remain and teach/research in Euro-American academic systems even with the knowledge that these systems are no better. It is a catch twenty-two situation where if one stays in Euro-American academic centers one is damned, and if one goes to the home country one is damned. Even worse, there is a huge brain drain from Majority World centers to Euro-American centers. Those who get tired and are disillusioned with tribal cocoons in the Majority World academic centers — their homes — just walk away and purchase a one-way ticket to Euro-American academic centers. For example in August 2015, the former South African president Thabo Mbeki said that since 1990, Africa has lost 20,000 academic professionals who left their countries to go work and live either in the USA or the UK.[122] And according to the International Organization for Migration, in the last quarter of a century Africa has lost one-third of its skilled personnel annually (doctors, lecturers, engineers, and other professionals) to waves of migration to North America and Western Europe.[123] Euro-American centers welcome these Majority World finest brains with open arms. After all aren't they the only ones who must have the best? In the end the very Majority World tribal enclaves that sustain academic tribalism end up marginalizing themselves by impoverishing their academic institutions through the loss of their finest brains. This is a tragedy that must be halted.

---

122. Africa News Agency, "The Extent of Africa's Brain Drain is 'Frightening': Mbeki," August 15, 2015, accessed January 20, 2016, https://www.enca.com/africa/extent-africa%E2%80%99s-brain-drain-frightening-mbeki.

123. Kigotho, "Are African universities ready for diaspora academics?"

In this book we are proposing a new hermeneutic, a new knowledge epistemology, one that liberalizes academia and saves it from the jaws of these unhealthy forces. We seek a knowledge epistemic system that allows for free and interdependent system of knowledge production, distribution, and consumption where all stakeholders work together. Our premise for making this proposal is that no one wins when certain knowledge and academicians are marginalized. The world becomes so much more academically impoverished when this happens to the extent that we all become the losers. Thus *knowledge activism* is a moral and ethical responsibility to our present world and the future generations of our children. We must all take our places and roles to empathize with each other for the common good and build a legacy of knowledge flow around the world without restrictions. This begins from the heart, from a personal commitment that arises out of the very nature of who we are as human beings — human beings bound together with a common fate of life in one planet hence the need for us to empathize with each other for our well-being. We demonstrate this empathy in the next section.

IV. CROSSROADS: WHEN MAJORITY AND MINORITY WORLD SCHOLARS MEET

R.S. Wafula & Joseph F. Duggan

A. Majority World Scholar: Intersections Between Empathy and *Knowledge Activism* — Wafula

How does one empathize with the Other? Where does the passion for empathy come from? In her book *A Postcolonial Woman's Encounter with Moses and Miriam* Angeline M.G. Song describes how her conflicted life and geopolitical-social transplantations become the impetus for her empathy. Song, a Singaporean woman of Chinese descent, was adopted by a single mother after her birth mother gave her up. Later in life she lived in France and then migrated to New Zealand. Through her adoption and translocated experiences, she came to personally understand what it means to be the Other. She understood and greatly appreciated the help she received from people of goodwill along the way. So as she reads the story of Moses and Miriam, (coincidentally Moses, like Song, was given up by his birth mother to "die" but was rescued and became adopted by Pharaoh's daughter) who are transplanted children (Israelites in imperializing Egypt) she empathizes with them and encounters their 'face.' In so doing she brings the story of Moses and Miriam in Exodus 2 to life for us (her readers), calling us to activate our empathy for others.[124] But as Song's reading illustrates empathy comes from the deep wells of our lives.

And here is my deep well. The better part of my life has been lived in company with marginality. My life's disadvantages began long before I was born. Just when my mother was in her early teens and in high school, she became pregnant. That pregnancy, which resulted in the birth of my elder sister, terminated my mother's schooling. For the next two or so years she hung on the hope that the man who had impregnated her would marry her — the best option for girls in her situation for the Kenya of her time. While she waited to get married she got pregnant again. That pregnancy resulted in my birth. The tragedy for me is that I was born with many health complications and was a sickly child throughout my first years of life. When I became of age my mother told me that I was a miracle child — a child of second chances. The recurrent sicknesses affected the growth rate of my right leg as compared to the left one to the extent that by the time I was five years old, I walked with a limp — and I still do. I was okay though until I started school. I remember in my early primary school years I was teased a lot by other kids because I could not run or play games that required fast movement. Sometimes the teasing degenerated into bullying where kids would strike me and run and then ask me to run after them and take revenge. I felt demeaned, isolated, and lonely. Inevitably I became introverted and kept to myself most of the time. When kids

---

124. Angeline M.G. Song, *A Postcolonial Woman's Encounter with Moses and Miriam* (New York, NY: Palgrave Macmillan, 2015). See chapter 1.

would go to play, I would either sit on the sides and watch them or just stay away.

Matters were made worse by other developments. My mother never got to marry the man who put her out of school. To her annoyance, the man went on to marry "another wife," sealing her fate as a single mother. Once this reality dawned on my mother her sixth sense — the sense of survival — kicked in. She decided to put my sister and me up with her relatives and try her hand at business. My sister went to live with our grandmother and I was taken in by an aunt — my mother's elder sister. Although most of my life at my aunt's home was great, and I will forever be grateful for the gesture of love she showed, there were many incidents when things happened that made me feel a sense of unbelonging. Take for example moments when I would go playing with my cousins — my aunt's children. If we got entangled into struggle, as kids always do, over something and we would go to my aunt for arbitration my aunt would more often than not rule in favor of her children (all mothers would probably do the same). Or take for example situations when my aunt returned from a journey, and we the children would run and hug her; I always got the last chance. So whereas my aunt's home gave me a place to stay, deep inside my young heart I was "homeless." I felt lonely and isolated. Again I resorted to *introvertism* as my escape. I would spend many hours just by myself. This worried my aunt. Oftentimes she would ask me what was wrong. The problem was that I couldn't dare explain how I felt. So my answer to her would often be that I missed my mom. On one of my mom's visits — and these were rare — I broke down and cried so uncontrollably that my mom could not bear it. She asked me what was wrong and I simply told her that I wanted to go with her. I was so insistent that she took me along.

My mother could not live with me because her business ventures got her travelling a lot. So she asked my grandmother who had taken in my sister to take me in too, and grandma agreed. I moved into grandma's home when I was thirteen years old and lived with her until when I turned twenty-four, got my first job, and moved out to live on my own. The years at my grandmother's home were the best years of my life. They were the best years not only because I got to live with my sister but also because our grandmother treated us really well. Having no children of her own, we became her children. As a matter of fact, we called her "Mom" rather than "Grandma," and she called us "my children" rather than "my grandchildren." But the years were also the most harrowing in terms of identity crises. I was growing up. I knew that I could not live with my grandma forever. I could not grow to build my own house in her compound. In other words, even when I had a roof over my head, I was still "homeless" at heart with no sense of rootedness and belonging. I worried a lot about my dark future. On the positive side, I had started working very hard at school. I knew that success in school was my only escape and hope for a good future life. At Sibumba Primary School in Chwele location and Bungoma District (as the administrative units were called then), I passed my primary school exams at the top of my class and joined Bungoma High School, in Bungoma town. Apparently my mother's business was doing very well and she paid for my school fees, at least for my first year of high school.

But as though fate had conspired against me, when I was in the second year of high school, my mother mysteriously disappeared and only reappeared long after I had finished high school and college. The circumstances and reasons for her disappearance are matters that belong to a story for another day. My mother's disappearance meant that I had no one to pay my fees for school. Although my grandmother would have done anything to keep me in school she did not have the financial means to do so. But she prayed every day for me. She reached out to all relatives, begging for help, sometimes with success, but most of the time without. She encouraged me to be strong and positive. I have recorded one of her memorable sentences to me in my first book which I dedicated to her and would repeat that sentence here as I would gladly do so a million other times in a million other places: "Young man, choices have either positive or negative consequences, and there is no positive consequence in giving up."[125] However, for a while her words did not withstand other much stronger forces. At the start of my junior year in high school, and with escalating unpaid fees, the head teacher called me one morning in his office and handed me a piece of paper that I have kept to date. The paper had these words: "You are a very smart child; you seem to have a bright future ahead of you. But I regret to have to inform you that you are deregistered from my school. We are not a charity school and need money to operate. And you have none to offer." I was very demoralized and remember weeping many days after that day. My only chance to a better life had slipped out of my hands. I stayed out of school for the whole of my junior high school year. The only thing that kept me alive — for I considered suicide several times — was my grandmother's word, "There is no positive consequence in giving up." With her words, I decided to keep reading. I reached out

---

125. Wafula, *Biblical Representations of Moab*, xiii.

to my former schoolmates for notes and read as though my life hung on understanding them.

During what would have been my senior year in high school my aunt (whom I had lived with as explained earlier) came, took me to the local education officer, and literally knelt down at his feet and begged him with tears to prevail on the headmaster of my high school to take me back so that I could sit for national exams. The officer was taken in with the "face" of my aunt and that of mine. He put us out of his office and had a closed door phone conversation with the headmaster. When he was done, he said, "Young man, I have taken a gamble on your life. The headmaster is willing to take you in on the condition that you can perform really well in your first term. He does not want your inferior performance to affect the school's national academic standing in the upcoming exams. If you do not come up among the top ten students, don't ever come to me for help." These words put me back to school. You can imagine the burden I carried on my shoulders for the education officer's gamble — which unknown to him was my gamble too. For two or so months nothing else mattered to me except reading. Miracle of all miracles! My efforts paid off. Even after missing almost two years of school, I emerged second in the examination results. That kept me in school and enabled me to sit for national exams. I passed my national exams among the top five students in my class. From then on miracle after miracle happened that enabled me to pay my way to college and later out of Kenya to graduate schools. Many people of goodwill, from different ethnicities and nationalities, in a design that is beyond my imagination, appeared in life and financially supported me along the way. Writing now as a PhD holder I can't agree more with my mom that indeed I am a miracle child.

These life experiences have given me a deep understanding of what it means to be on the margins of life as well as appreciation of how things can change if people of goodwill come to the aid of marginalized people. For me, therefore, to stand up for the marginalized Other is not a mere academic endeavor. It is rather an existential value that calls me to pay forward the debt I owe many of my past benefactors. The marginalized are a part of me. They are me. Their pain is my personal pain too. The thing is, when you have been marginalized the better part of your life you become so intimately familiar with how marginalization works that detecting it takes not much effort. Smith speaks my heart when she states that marginalization hurts so much that it saturates one's songs, stories, and everyday routines.[126] For me, this saturation makes marginalization a burden that I can't unload and pretend it doesn't exist. My marginalization and that of others makes me apprehensive and alert creating a passionate desire within me end it.

However, I do not think you have to be born in a Majority World country and experience the misery like mine to be able to empathize with the Other. In a way we are all products of empathy. It is a quality that germinates in every human being regardless of geopolitical, social locations, and economic status as the story of my co-author, below, will amply illustrate. Because of the nature of our humanness we all grow up accumulating along the way what I call vulnerability zones. Think for example about the following conditions. When you were a little baby, you were completely dependent on your parents or guardians for everything. Because of their goodwill (not of course discounting in some circumstances the negative formations) you grew to be the person you are. Or think about those

---

126. Smith, *Decolonizing Methodologies*, 20.

moments when you were really sick. You pinned all your get-well hope on the medical professional(s) or your caretakers. Better still, and closer to academia, think about your graduate school years. You needed someone to pay your fees, or take care of your family/business. You needed some professor who believed in you and took you in. Indeed, I have never met or heard any PhD graduate who can honestly say that they did it on their own. And the list can go on and on. When you think about these vulnerable zones, you realize that you do not need to go too far away to encounter the "face." It is right there before you. If someone came along and helped you to become the person you turned out to be, how can you retreat comfortably into your personal space and not worry about others who need help? In this book we are appealing for our concerted efforts to help Majority World scholars participate fully in the economy of knowledge production, distribution, and consumption. In a later chapter we will explain our praxes and hope you can encounter the 'face' within you and within others and come alongside me and my co-author (whose story follows next) to change the world.

B. Minority World Scholarship — Duggan

There are many paths to *knowledge activism*. Activism is never authorized and rarely desired by those who have privileged access. *Knowledge activism* is experienced through education. Wafula was raised in Kenya through his undergraduate years with his masters and doctoral work in Scotland and the United States and continuing through the challenges he met to publish his first book. My path is through being raised in the United States and eventually meeting Wafula at a Postcolonial Networks meeting in Kenya at St. Paul's University in May 2014. While we each have lived in geographically, religiously, economically, ethnically, and racially diverse contexts, we share the same passions, values and commitments. We are both well read in the literature, but the literature has not and cannot lead to decolonize knowledge. Decolonial knowledge is liberated knowledge that cannot submit to the narrow, racial contours of the academy and publishing. Decolonial knowledge cannot be coopted.

In both of our stories our voices were partially silenced and sometimes refused the privilege to be heard. We both know the struggle to be heard. While there are substantial differences between the two of us given my white privilege, the colonial knowledge economy negatively impacts all actors in different ways. Wafula speaks eloquently about the way privilege and marginalization are not so easily compartmentalized in ways that would otherwise separate our experiences of education. As adults we also learned firsthand from major publishers whose *knowledge activism* must be an ethical priority. Although our stories are different we met at a crossroads, and now we are working towards a common vision that enables us to dare to rethink the privileges to be published, read, cited and influence change.

An Unfolding Autobiographical Path to Knowledge Activism

Our beliefs are shaped by our experience. It was no accident when I brought together the words *knowledge* and *activism* to name ways that knowledge is decolonized. We did not "discover" *knowledge activism*. People have been practicing *knowledge activism* without our labeling of the terms *knowledge activism* and *knowledge activist*. As noted in our Foreword, Gloria Anzaldúa was a *knowledge activist* writing decades before she sought a PhD or the University of California Santa Cruz granted her a doctorate after her death. Ngũgĩ Wa Thiong'o was a *knowledge activist* when he questioned the place of African literature in the dominant knowledge system. Both authors published with small independent presses where their work was accessible to many readers.

Aunt Lute Press was a youthful press when they organized to support multicultural, feminist women's voices and published Anzaldúa. According to Aunt Lute's website, the press was established in 1982 in Iowa City by Barb Weiser and Joan Pinkvoss "who believed that neither mainstream publishing nor the feminist movement of that time was promoting the voices of lesbians, especially lesbians and women of color." Aunt Lute continues to be a Press of "voices of women from many different cultures." The Aunt Lute story is not an exception to the experience of marginalized scholars who find presses for their voices to be heard. Both of these authors' books are still available today at reasonable prices. In this book we hope to encourage more people to follow in the prophetic footsteps of Anzaldúa, Aunt Lute Press and Wa Thiong'o when every researcher, scholar, librarian, publisher and reader finds ways to practice a *knowledge activism* mindset. Then together we will energize decolonial knowledge that subverts dominant knowledge.

My journey to become a *knowledge activist* was unplanned and yet in an existential sense has been unfolding over the course of my entire life and continues through this book and the actions of Borderless Press and Postcolonial Networks. With a difficult birth that placed my mother's life and mine at great risk, I take strength from the word of God in Jeremiah 1: "Before I formed you in the womb I knew you, before you were born I set you apart; I appointed you as a prophet to the nations." A lifetime of formal education that began as a preschooler with a stutter, a precocious teenager, intensified during my masters and doctorate and took shape in my post-doctorate experiences with social media and my awareness of the blinding limits of major academic publishing collectively led to my development to become a *knowledge activist*.

I cannot develop an argument about the way I have been led to *knowledge activism* through existing scholarly literature because I have not, though many postcolonial inspired books have contributed to my formation as a *knowledge activist*. As a *knowledge activist* my passions have been formed primarily through my observation and direct experience of gaps between theory and praxis, reflection and my ongoing disappointment that knowledge tables are predominantly homogenous in composition.

One year Postcolonial Networks invited several scholars to write "postcolonial body performance narratives" (PBPN). We offered the PBPN genre as a way to invite autobiographical accounts that delved deeper than mere articulation of postcolonial principles in ways that demonstrated the way people were practicing the principles. Our hope was to amplify the postcolonial principles in ways that compelled inspiration, modeling and activism. In PBPNs authors could write in the first person where they first experienced marginalization before they read critical theory principles. It is in this sense that I write in this chapter following the PBPN style to show the inception of my postcolonial yearnings that have continued to unfold, evolve and deepen in ways that have led to my *knowledge activism*.

The Struggle and Gift to Speak

My parents and family recognized that I had a speech impediment when I was only five years old. I could not pronounce polysyllabic words. I reduced all polysyllabic words to monosyllabic words. So I called my sister Mary, "Mare"; Billy, "Bil"; Kathy "Kat"; and Jimmy, "Jim". I was brought to a speech therapist who would teach me how to speak without stuttering. I spent at least one summer going to speech therapy lessons all morning, every day at Mount Saint Ursula Academy in New York City where I visited Sr. Winifred, an Ursuline Sister and then-famous speech therapist.

Many years later in college in a final exam in a speech class, after giving an impromptu speech I was asked to stay after class to speak with my speech teacher, Fr. James Conlan. Fr. Conlan said, "May I ask you a personal question?" "Yes of course," I said. He continued and asked me, "As a child did you see Sr. Winifred for speech therapy?" Stunned for a few seconds by his apparent clairvoyant skills, I then said, "Yes, but how do you know?" Fr. Conlan said, "Sr. Winifred left her signature on your tongue." I asked "And what does that signature look like?" Fr. Conlan responded, "I am afraid I cannot tell you for if I did there would be at great risk that Sr. Winfred's work would be erased and your stutter would return."

All throughout elementary school my reading comprehension scores were substantially below those of my peers. After years of being ignored and left isolated in overcrowded classrooms, in seventh grade my parents found a reading tutor for me who taught me to read. In less than a year my reading comprehension dramatically improved though too late to have an impact on my acceptance rate into academically strong high school programs. I attended a high school for academically challenged students that specialized in small classes and individual tutors continuing my journey to recognize the potential of my voice.

IV. Crossroads: When Majority and Minority World Scholars Meet • R.S. Wafula & Joseph F. Duggan

I recall in high school being alarmed by the way fellow students coveted their bibliographies and rarely shared them with me, or others in class. Bibliographies were protected as if they provided the solution to humanity's greatest questions. In college I continued to see the bibliography protected by those who created them. In my youth I knew that resistance to sharing bibliographies and later books is a serious moral, ethical assault on humanity. Although I graduated with honors from my high school it would not be until many years later that I would identify and pursue my academic passions rather than following a familial seeded duty of being educated to prepare for a career. In a rather sporadic and iterative learning maturation process I gradually came to ask questions that led me to small research projects and extensive periods of reading on a subject of interest.

My lifelong passion is power analysis — who has voice and who does not; who is at the table and who is not; who has power over others and who is powerless to others; who has the privilege to follow their dreams and whose dreams are ignored or rejected? Over a two-decade period during a time of intense spiritual formation (1987–2010) my passions led me to read liberation, black, feminist, womanist, queer, postcolonial theologies and critical theories. In 1987 I studied at General Theological Seminary (Episcopal) under Dr. Richard Schaull, Visiting Professor from Princeton University who mentored me in liberation theology especially in the works of Leonardo Boff, Jon Sobrino and Pablo Richard.

At the Episcopal Divinity School (EDS) and also in the Boston Theological Institute I was encouraged to pursue a masters and a doctorate. EDS further strengthened my commitment to social justice and anti-oppression methodologies with a passion for postcolonial and liberation work. At the University of Manchester my doctoral thesis continued to delve into postcolonial principles but the most important impact on my doctorate was the experience in supervision. My doctoral supervisor challenged me to connect my research and writing to international communities through engaged dialogue with many different people and perspectives.

Initial Recognition of the Knowledge System and Its Privileges

It was during the course of my doctoral research that I began to observe some disturbing characteristics of my research. Initially these research characteristics lacked a pattern that only later did I begin to recognize after multiple observations. At the center of a multicultural university I was acutely aware of polyvocality and as a result I began to more quickly see gaps between critical theories' emphasis on multiplicity and the majority of published research. The first thing I noticed in many theology and critical theory books was that citations were routinely for North American and European presses and scholars. Majority World scholars from Africa, Asia and South America were cited only on an exception basis. I began to look for books by Majority World scholars on Amazon and other online stores, but quickly realized that online bookstores promoted segmented knowledge cultures that kept scholars around the globe apart.

As I read the work of radical scholars I observed their rigorous critique of the corporate military industrial complex coupled with their complicit participation in the system they critiqued by publishing their books with presses that priced their books in ways that only a small portion of the world's population have the privilege to read. Even with rapidly decreasing tenure positions, retired faculty not being replaced with new faculty and dramatically increasing adjunct lecturer positions, academics are still hungry for prestige academic brands to publish their work. Every generation of academic seems oblivious to the severe market fragmentation that privileges Western scholarship with an unrecognized bias against Majority World scholarship. Almost every literature review is incomplete in the absence of Majority World scholarship, but doctoral chairs never reject the masters or doctoral project for the way masters and doctoral candidates fail to address scholarly work from the Majority World.

All of these observations clarified the needs to decolonize knowledge and informed my role in offering leadership to change the system. I brought together twenty years of business experience and twenty years reading radical theologies and theories as I made a commitment to be an ally with Majority World scholars. At EDS students were invited to ally with, advocating side-by-side to enable institutional change to foster justice through anti-oppression praxis. During the course of my PhD work I did not feel called to be a scholar or published academic but increasingly to anti-oppression praxis. In those days the words *knowledge activism* and *knowledge activist* were still far from my consciousness.

"I found space for my voice here."
As my doctoral research continued, Dr. Peter Scott, my doctoral supervisor encouraged me to organize an international meeting as part of my research formation. The meeting held in May 2008 at the University of Manchester complemented my research on postcolonial ecclesiological questions across the Anglican Communion. Scholars came to the meeting from Africa, Asia, Australia, North America

and Europe. Unlike many academic meetings where scholars give lengthy papers with short responses and then leave the meeting, we developed a different meeting culture. We offered several opportunities for informal conversations and interdisciplinary panels to further explore the formal work of the conference.

At the end of the meeting, the Rev. Dr. David Joy, Professor of New Testament at United Theological College in Bangalore, India exclaimed: "I found space for my voice here!" Joy's words may have been the most consciousness-shaping words of my entire PhD program. His words led me through the supervision of my doctoral supervisor to launch "Divinity After Empire", a series of meetings around the world especially in Global South — Majority World contexts. Joy's vision led to his and other Majority World scholars' collaborations with the Lincoln Theological Institute at the University of Manchester and Postcolonial Networks. Meetings have been held in Bangalore, India in January 2010; Melbourne, Australia in January 2012; in Limuru, Kenya in May 2014; and again in Manchester in May 2016 where the focus was on multiple faiths living side by side in postcolonial cities.

At each meeting contextual concerns with global resonances were engaged by local scholars as well as a few others visiting from around the world. The primary focus of these meetings was to meet in Majority World contexts where scholars who often are financially impeded from attendance at scholarly meetings in North America and Europe were able to not only attend but also lead these meetings and publish their papers in books they edited. Every meeting led to the publication of a series of firsts with scholarship authored and edited by Majority World scholars in Global South contexts.

Global Network and Knowledge Sharing

Due to the energy created by the Manchester meeting several scholars had the desire to stay in conversation and so a group called the Postcolonial Theology Network was formed on Facebook in September 2008. While the group began with a few people from the Manchester meeting, very quickly the group began to grow in numbers and scope of postcolonial concerns.

In the first few years the group developed a distinctive reputation for being a place where people gathered, exchanged information and participated in energetic discussions. An online group culture was quickly fostered where a multiplicity of voices were heard in contrast to the often polarizing culture of many Facebook groups. Through this group it was not unusual for scholars, activists, and pastors to become friends with people across race, class and economic differences. With so much diversity and volume of threads I began to invite members to write on particular questions, write essays and or book reviews with scheduled respondents to keep the group stimulated on a weekly basis. Publishers respected the PTN so much that they regularly offered review copies of new books and I would ask members to write reviews for the PTN. With growing number of PTN readers we surpassed the subscriber base of most academic journals.

The PTN is one of only 200–300 Facebook groups with 10,000+ members. Unfortunately, the diversification of the group throughout the Majority World has been very limited. Some Majority World scholars found their way to the group especially from India. However, North American and European white men often dominated the online conversations. The shape of the conversations was too often oriented on North American questions, concerns and ways of thinking. Rarely did members outside North America or Europe initiate conversations. North American and European social segmentation often easily hijacked the group as they reframed Majority World concerns into dominant Minority World concerns. As the group grew larger it became less and less clear what postcolonial meant. The word postcolonial became synonymous with white, liberal and progressive commitments in ways that dramatically narrowed conversations from our broader inclusive vision.

After many failed attempts to diversify the composition of the group, I made it a requirement that I pre-approve all posts. The pre-approval process for posts also overlapped with our shift to an exclusive focus on knowledge activism. Postcolonial Networks also has a page with approximately over 1000 likes. I considered closing the PTN, but it has throughout the years been an excellent source of networking for so many people around the world. Through the PTN I became more aware and alert that when North Americans and Europeans are mixed in with people from the Majority World, the white males will take over the conversation to the exclusion of people of color, especially those from colonized nations.

The Facebook group in part led to the launching of Postcolonial Networks, a 501c3 not-for-profit. The tax-free designation was granted in July 2012. The initial vision was to foster communities to promote postcolonial knowledge through conferences, journals and books published by Majority World scholars. It took the better part of a decade as an organization to figure out our mission doing one thing well. Our decade-long development is briefly delineated into three phases of activities:

1. International meetings and publication in edited collections through Palgrave

2. Journals and open access
3. Borderless Press

***Knowledge Activism* Within the Existing Knowledge System: Palgrave**

Postcolonial Networks' development is seen through our impact within the established knowledge production system — and also, in a move beyond the institution through Borderless Press. Working within the existing knowledge system the *Postcolonialism and Religions* series was established to publish scholarship that brings together theory and theology with eighty percent Majority World scholars as authors. The series has been a huge success meeting our founding vision goal for the composition of authors. J. Jayakiran Sebastian, co-editor and a Postcolonial Networks board member emphasizes the importance of Majority World scholars being published by a major academic press such as Palgrave Macmillan. The series has over a dozen volumes having only been established in the summer of 2012. One of the other early visions of the series was to make the books available to scholars around the world at affordable prices. We have never been able to bring this vision of more affordable economics to readers in Majority World nations.

Palgrave taught me about the rigors and process of academic publishing. I learned the process from initial submission of a book proposal through all the steps including double-blind peer review, copyediting and layout. While our series continues to be a success, at the same time, Postcolonial Networks had great difficulty articulating a clear and coherent vision of its mission. With the assistance of Melody Stanford, a communications and branding consultant, we worked out a clear definition of our path forward eventually leading to our *knowledge activism* and our focus on Borderless Press. The story of the development of Postcolonial Networks and Borderless Press is long and complex enough to justify a dedicated volume. My purpose here is to chronicle the insights and stages of development that kept us moving forward towards our *knowledge activism* mission.

Knowledge Activism Within the Existing Knowledge System: Journals

Concurrent with development of the Palgrave series, Postcolonial Networks made an effort to establish two postcolonial journals. While the journals were initiated to serve Majority World scholars whose work is often rejected by prestigious peer review journals, it became challenging to draw contributions from the Majority World contexts and at the same time receive support from readers around the world. The journals could not avoid a bifurcation of the scholarly market between Majority World scholars and those in North America and Europe. Faculty and tenure committees in North America frowned upon submission of papers to independent journals such as ours and it was difficult to establish our credibility. As the founding editor it was necessary for me to learn firsthand the politics of publishing and the ways the academy keeps apart the Majority World contributions from those of North Americans and Europeans.

Postcolonial Networks' reputation for quality scholarship afforded us the opportunity to associate with a major academic publisher but if we made that decision our Majority World author contributors and their higher education institutions likely would not have been able to afford our journal. Postcolonial Networks chose to close the journal until *knowledge activism* progressed sufficiently for all scholars to share the same space.

Knowledge Activism — The Break Away from Institutions: Borderless Press

Borderless Press' vision from day one has been to publish Majority World authors and their scholarship. How we do this has evolved through our ongoing learning of the system of injustice that often remains invisible in the academy and among major academic publishers. I readily admit my own naïveté that Borderless Press could streamline the production process, remove the cost, and return significant royalties to our Majority World authors.

On a small scale we did remove the cost to publish a high-quality book that met the rigors of double-blind peer review, but we did not plan that without a distribution strategy few would purchase our books. Even though the books were reasonably priced, the books were not included in syllabi even by editors and their contributors. Even though we have a global social media presence, our books did not move into broader readership. Majority World scholarship is not sought-after scholarship due to the extensive institutional biases and barriers towards acceptance.

We initially published books at a total cost of just over one thousand dollars because we lacked the overhead costs associated with major publishing houses' systems of production, and we benefitted from extraordinary contributions of substantially below-market fees by copy editors and production editors. Our fixed costs were for copyediting and production. We were able to do this by working with per diem copy editors and production editors. Our costs escalated in our second year for two reasons. First, as we learned that our authors couldn't make it through the double-blind peer review process because they lack the time and access to scholarly resources. Early on, one scholar's manuscript was read by one of the most senior scholars in the field. This particular peer reviewer scholar had finished two peer reviews at about the same time. One peer review was returned to a North American scholar who completed all the revisions necessary in a period of two to three months. The Majority World scholar said that she could not address her revisions for probably several years. The second reason our costs escalated is because our volume of authors dramatically increased, but without sales we could not compensate per diem copy editors and production editors.

We quickly learned that while our book publishing process followed the same academic rigors of major publishing houses and although we were able to publish at the fraction of the cost of major publishers, our *knowledge activist* interventions were not complete. To address lack of time for rewriting and addressing peer review revisions we instituted a residency program where with our higher education partners (currently Drew University, Luther College, and Eden Theological Seminary) bring some of our Majority World authors scholars to the United States to work with an assigned scholar mentor, access to library resources and accommodations. Most of the costs associated with the residency are covered by our partner institutions and in some cases supplemented by Postcolonial Networks.

At the end of the writing and publishing residency, the author will be in a more competitive place as the privileged North American and European authors who often have the privilege to work with a senior scholar in their department and have the benefit of a pre-peer review before the formal and official double-blind peer review process. These North American and European authors often fly through the double-blind peer review and receive the coveted assessment "publish without revision" because they have benefitted from an equivalent scholar who routinely completes double-blind peer reviews. Our publishing process seeks to imitate this embedded closed intellectual knowledge system process. Unlike major publishers we make major investments in our authors' development from the outset of the project bringing together all the resources that make the Majority World author's project competitive.

Initially we naively believed that our books would rapidly sell in North America, Europe and in the Majority World. We quickly learned that our cost savings and investment in Majority World scholarship would not change the closed intellectual knowledge system. Our Majority World authors are immersed in a culture that purchases one book for the library, and students access that one book rather than purchase their own copy. So far North American and European faculty have for the most part ignored the publication of our books because of an inherited colonial bias against Majority World scholarship. I would argue that brand has very little to do with the books that are purchased. The primary drive is an institutional bias against Majority World scholarship. Borderless Press has failed to sell our books due to the deep economic biases of the closed intellectual knowledge based system readers. The exact same manuscript with the imprint of a major publishing house would benefit from the recurring institutional sales and scholars with their articles and books would find these authors' works in their university library.

It is through these impediments that Postcolonial Networks is finding necessary additional *knowledge activist* interventions that pierce the closed intellectual knowledge based system to promote its Borderless Press authors' scholarship. We have come to see the book no longer as a commodity to be sold but rather as an invitation to conversation and *knowledge activist* change. Commodities are driven by cost-benefits, profits and losses. Commodities by definition satisfy a want or need and are offered through a process of economic exchange. When and if there is an unrecognized need, then there is a need for a different knowledge activist intervention rather than offering a more price-efficient commodity. Marx anticipated that there are needs that defy economic value exchange that are common to all humans. Yet if there is no recognized value or what Marx called "exchange-value," then production remains dormant or nonexistent. In his book, *Critical Strategies for Social Research*, William Carroll argues that the condition of poverty is when human needs fail to be met by available commodities.[127]

The closed intellectual knowledge system whose access has been carefully managed by knowledge insiders has effectively produced global knowledge poverty. To pierce the system of exchange that otherwise occludes Majority World scholarship and Majority World authors we need to leave behind the capitalist system of production for publishing knowledge. The major academic publishers and their privileged customers at the top five hundred research libraries have little motivation or desire to disrupt global knowledge poverty as they benefit greatly from these inequities despite their critical Marxist arguments published by prestige publishers. The law of supply and demand drives the price of the book commodity and secures limited access

---

127. W. Carroll, *Critical Strategies for Social Research* (Toronto: Canadian Scholars Press, 2004).

to knowledge in ways that assure its continued justification of exorbitant book prices with desired profits.

Borderless Press is now in the enviable position that we have proof of concept that our small independent press has a process to publish high-quality scholarship. Going into our third year we have accepted ten authors from our partner university, St. Paul's, just outside of Nairobi where for two years we have held a five-day workshop to coach and mentor PhDs in scholarly writing and publishing. We have invitations to do our writing and publishing workshop in Uganda, Tanzania and New Delhi. The only impediment that impedes scaling Borderless Press to become a higher volume publisher is voluntary scholars, copy editors and production staff to support our process. In the meantime, we have to pace our publication of books with our available resources. We are confident that once our Majority World scholarship is purchased at the same rate of other scholarship we will be able to convert from a voluntary based organization to a financially sustainable organization. The impediment to sustainability is not the lack of Majority World scholars or a publisher who promotes Majority World scholarship. The primary impediments are readers, libraries and faculty who take seriously Majority World authors and their scholarship.

V. *KNOWLEDGE ACTIVISM* AFTER THEORY

R.S. Wafula & Joseph F. Duggan

A. The Way *Knowledge Activism* Theory Becomes Praxis — Duggan

Almost every week on my Facebook page I see scholars make the announcement of their long-awaited new book published by a major academic publisher. These new book announcements follow a lockstep pattern that few authors notice, question, resist, challenge, or break free.

 The publication of a scholarly book represents years of research and writing by an author-scholar. The newly published book does not just represent the brilliance of the author but also insights gained from doctoral faculty, fellow scholars who served as readers, and also the recommendations of double-blind peer reviewers. The book is also the result of a meticulous copy editor; a cover artist and the pride of back cover endorsers. Friends of the author cannot wait to see and read the book! Then when the book is announced all of this great anticipation is dashed when the cost of the book is $80 USD, $125USD or as much as $160USD! With no desire to shame authors who are colleagues and friends I encourage readers to go to the websites of Ashgate, Cambridge University Press, Oxford University Press, Palgrave Macmillan, and Routledge to confirm the above book prices across all disciplines and out of reach to most scholars especially those in the Majority World.

When Scholars Look the Other Way — Duggan
Interspersed among the flurry of Facebook posts are a few friends and friends of friends who register a complaint at the high cost of the book. Books that emphasize anti-imperial theories, postcolonial works, and decolonial visions appropriately receive an even greater number of critiques for the book's price given the way the price is out of step with the anti-oppression vision of the books. The above pattern repeats week after week on every scholar's Facebook page with no end in sight. Authors often see themselves as victims of corporate publishers that need to make a profit to recover their costs to publish. Yet very few scholars have taken a bold *knowledge activist* stand and if necessary publish through independent presses that often come with a far less costly price tag. The first priority of the author is to choose a well-established publisher that will be well regarded by tenure committees. Rarely does a scholar question the knowledge production practices of their desired publisher or university and even less common is the Gloria Anzaldúa-kind of scholar whose writing matches their choice of publisher.

Similarly, publishers have not changed the knowledge production system. Publishers would be quick to describe the way they are challenged by the high cost of production and razor-thin profit margins. Publishers have an opportunity to reduce cost of books through more affordable technologies. However, publishers typically see reduced internal cost as a means to increase their profit and offer slightly reduced priced books but not sufficient to attract most scholar reader budgets.

Editors and marketing managers diligently ask if a particular book will sell to their readers. Marketing researchers at every major publishing house track readers' preferences and pass along the results of their research to editorial boards. These editorial boards advise the editor to go back to the author to change the book's title to be more easily searchable in scholarly research databases or change the cover art to be a better sell. In some cases, while the book received a stellar recommendation of double-blind peer reviewers the publisher's editorial board feels the need to reject the book because they fear the book will not sell and they will incur a loss on the publication of the book! Or worse they make the author pay hefty fees to cover for the publication costs at the expense of the author rather than on themselves.

The major consumers are institutional buyers at the major research libraries around the world. Libraries are not committed to change the knowledge production system to include Majority World scholars. The academy and its canonical disciplines greatly influence if not actually determine the production of major academic publishers. Often I have heard academic publishers attempt to categorize cutting-edge scholarship into existing canonical disciplines and when they cannot then they determine that the book will not sell and therefore cannot be published. There is a major disconnect between innovative scholarship and what sells. Readers are deprived of an even greater wealth of information due to profit-driven decision-making at the major publishers.

When Faculty Teach Privilege — Duggan

Universities teach doctoral researchers how to ask research questions, make methodological decisions, develop a literature review, shape an argument and draw conclusions. The most fortunate newly minted scholars in the Minority World have the privilege of scholar-mentors who assist the first-time author make their dissertation into a book. Newly minted PhDs venture off to the annual American Academy of Religion meeting or other professional meeting and market their book to a host of publishers. Even more privileged and fortunate authors are introduced to a publisher by a senior faculty member who wisely wants to make sure that the author's manuscript does not get lost in the publishing maze.

All the other new PhDs, particularly scholars from the Majority World, are on their own to identify a publisher who might be interested enough in their book to publish it. Nowhere in their doctoral studies or after the defense were these scholar authors coached on the way to pitch their book to available publishers. Although these authors have read books through their undergraduate, graduate and post-graduate studies, most are innocent of the market realities of publishing. These scholars — even the most privileged among them — lack scholar mentors to advise them on these realities. The dominant taught pattern in the scholarly community is to ask a research question, write a book, publish with a credible academic publisher and begin the plan to write your next book.

Credible publishers are those publishers whose imprint will carry the expected weight of sufficient points in a tenure application in the scholar's discipline. Due to the secrecy of the publishing process, particularly the economics of publishing most academics are not knowledgeable enough to make informed decisions as consumers of intellectual knowledge. The top academic publishers prey on the innocence of scholar authors. The largest academic corporate publishers are deeply integrated into the corporate-industrial complex that many authors critique in their books but fail to realize that their publisher is also a part of it. Nor as already noted above do many authors accept their privilege and complicit role in the corporate publishing machine that is integrally connected to their discipline's lack of *knowledge activist* leadership to embody their anti-oppression theory in affordable books for all to read.

Reactive Responses to Invisible Publishers — Duggan
The way that publishers are able to remain profitable is to outsource the vast majority of their book production process. The publisher through an editor is most active at three points in the publishing process: acquisition of the title, double-blind peer review assignment and presentation of the peer reviewer's recommendation to publish to the publisher's editorial board. These three steps are the least time consuming and least costly steps in the entire production and publishing of the book. The most time-consuming and labor intensive steps are the least-compensated and least-valued steps. The double-blind peer reviewer, if they are lucky, will receive $150 or so for reading the proposed book manuscript and taking the time to write helpful comments to the publisher that are eventually sent to the author. All other quality control steps in the process are either the responsibility of junior editorial assistants who are in their roles often for less than two years and who may be in their first job out of undergraduate programs; an offshore company that manages the layout including proofs, and the author who must identify back cover endorsers, present cover art or go with baseline covers and recommend

journals for book reviews. In contrast Borderless Press has PhDs working with our authors at every step in the publication process.

Most major academic publishers need not spend a lot of time on marketing, as they are able to cover their costs and make a profit on every book through their repeating customers at the major research libraries who have standing orders. A decade ago I was at a preaching conference at National Cathedral in Washington, DC and I had the privilege to dine every morning with Dr. John Polkinghorne. He was visiting Washington National Cathedral to talk about one of his newest books. One morning at breakfast I naively asked Dr. Polkinghorne if he was traveling with his publisher and he told me that in the past publishers marketed authors' books. Now and for more than a decade publishers list new books in their annual or quarterly catalog and show the book at that year's academic meetings. Another scholar told me the way his new book proudly shown at one professional meeting and then the following year his book was thrown in a pile of previous years published books like a pair of discounted shoes in Filene's Basement Department Store in Boston![128]

Polkinghorne and this scholar exercise prudent judgment in the realization that they must take primary responsibility to make sure their book is not forgotten. The primary way academic books are not forgotten is through the process of citations. The most successful books are authors' whose works are cited in other scholars' books. Ideally these cita-

---

128. The article in the following website lays out clearly the narrative behind the unhealthy publisher practices that prey on a scholar's work motivated primarily with capitalistic financial gains (See Academics Anonymous, "Academics are being hoodwinked into writing books nobody can buy," *Guardian*, September 4, 2015, accessed September 10 2016, https://www.theguardian.com/higher-education-network/2015/sep/04/academics-are-being-hoodwinked-into-writing-books-nobody-can-buy).

tions are in the most respected peer-reviewed journals as these citations generally count more than many citations in books by unknown authors. In tenure applications at many universities it is important to have the requisite first book and even better two books published by prestigious publishers, but the major tenure differentiator is several peer-reviewed articles with multiple citations of the article in other peer-reviewed journals.

Impermeable Resistance to Change — Duggan
In summary I have offered this condensed overview of the challenges of publishing to point to some of the reasons why authors, publishers, libraries, faculty, and readers have not been able to change the knowledge production system that impedes access to published scholarship. The result of this dominant capitalist model of book publishing is that it privileges very few scholars — most often heteronormative men located in North America and Europe.

Editorial boards are filled with academics from universities in North America, the United Kingdom and Europe. We see this most clearly in discipline areas where content should be coming from Majority World scholars and Majority World universities. For example, in the African Studies of the Oxford Bibliographies, the Editor-in-Chief is Professor Emeritus at the University of Wisconsin-Madison. The standing editorial board of six scholars has one scholar who received his PhD from the University of Nairobi. The founding editorial board of twelve scholars has only two scholars with their graduation education from universities in Africa. The most telling picture is the composition of contributors for articles. With well over one hundred plus contributions in the African Studies section of the Oxford Bibliographies website, less than ten percent of the contributions were written by scholars from universities in Africa! Most of those selected to write are from South Africa and very rarely from Central or East Africa.

Many of the major academic publishers will not accept peer reviewers from outside North America or Europe. The preferred double-blind peer reviewers also have posts at major research universities in North America and Europe. My reader homework assignment for you is to go to your favorite North American or European academic press' website and count the number of authors or members of editorial boards or consulting scholars from Africa, Asia or South America. Occasionally you will find a scholar from a university in South Africa, but infrequently will you see scholars from leading universities in other parts of Africa or other parts of the Majority World. The intellectual knowledge network is closed and tightly managed by professors on major faculties and publishers in North America and Europe for their exclusive benefit. You can further confirm the existence of this closed network by the pattern of citations as reciprocal benefit to those scholars within this closed network.

Economic Realities Behind the Scenes

Based on some anecdotal information the cost to publish an academic book at a major university press or corporate academic publisher in North America and Europe ranges from $5000–$8000 (in US dollars) per published book. From three hundred and fifty to five hundred research libraries around the world will purchase each book from a major publisher. At $80–$125 per volume on an average of 425 books sold, the publisher's gross sales are $34,000 to $53,125. When the publisher recovers its $5000–8000 publishing costs, the net sales is $29,000 to $45,125. These figures seem very high and one would think as adequate profit, but these dollars contribute to their major infrastructure costs that include human resources: for example, editor salaries at an average of $45,000 per year, benefits, legal, insurance, taxes, systems and more. Editors typically are responsible for the acquisition and publication of eighty to one hundred volumes each year. Editors spend the majority of their time managing the internal processes that lead to publication. Publishers are faced with increased competition from alternative technologies including open-access publishing and diminished institutional research library budgets as universities increasingly cut budgetary corners, becoming even more selective in their purchase of books.

Universities rate publishing brands as credible beyond all others because of the heightened level of confidence that these books have been through the highest levels of academic rigor before the book is published. Universities don't have the time to assess the exceptions to the corporate publishing machine. There may be other outstanding books that are published by high-quality, start-up, independent presses, but these are not likely to secure the same number of points in tenure applications. It becomes a vicious cycle that justifies the prestigious publisher as the expected baseline producing questions about why an author chose a smaller independent press versus choosing to be published by a major academic publisher. Clearly all if they had the opportunity, they would choose the most prestigious recognized brand than make an informed decision to go with a smaller press. Some of these independent presses may be closer to the author's values and the book's arguments, but that is weighed far lower in personal value than the institution's approval of their scholarship especially when the scholar is on the tenure track.

Reader assignment: Take a break from reading and pull a North American or European published book off your office shelf and thumb through the bibliography and footnotes. Whose names do you see in the bibliography and footnotes and whose names do you not see? Who is not at the publishing table? Whose work is not valued enough to appear in this important new book?

Majority World Authors Left Without Good Choices
In many Majority World contexts, scholars are left with no other publishing avenues than the option to locally print their book project. These authors closed out of the intellectual knowledge system lack access to the publishing resources to have their manuscript go through the double-blind peer review process. As North American and European scholars are innocent to the internal publishing house processes, so also are most Majority World scholars. Unlike their North American and European counterparts, these Majority World scholars absent from the table lack the power to subvert the dominant publishing system. Their scholarship remains local and out of view and reach of citations.

Many Majority World scholars choose to print their books through a local press in Bangalore, Buenos Aires or Nairobi. These authors will often pay to have their book printed in a print run of 100 to 1000 copies. Often these authors will pay as much as $2000USD to have their book printed. The book will be in local shops proximate to the print shop and maybe one copy finds their way to the scholar's local university, but these books will never reach the eyes of scholars doing research in North America, Europe and other parts of the world. These very same authors as Wafula argued were raised on the scholarship of North Americans and Europeans. A few like Wafula find an opportunity to have their book published in North America and some will pay dearly for the privilege by also paying the publisher a sum of $3000–$5000 to publish their book. These publishers doubt the quality of the Majority World author's book and refuse to risk inadequate sales, so they make certain to cover their costs and profit upfront. The author sees no return and if lucky receives a small royalty check when the book begins to sell through institutional sales.

There is no postcolonial or decolonial knowledge without dramatically changing the ways knowledge is created, produced and distributed. The dominant knowledge creation, production, and distribution system is colonial. It has been my intent in this chapter to demonstrate that publishing houses and universities cannot be scapegoated as the only responsible actors. It is imperative for individual scholars: authors and readers that seek justice through anti-oppression to make disruptive choices that subvert the dominant knowledge production system. The *knowledge activism* we present in this book offers you the means to begin your *knowledge activism* so that together we might foster a worldwide movement of change.

B. *Knowledge Activism* Cartography: Workshop, Pre-peer Review, Scholar Mentor, Writing Residency, Peer Review, Publishing, Alternate Readings Lenses, Economics — Wafula

Major Euro-American Publishers: A Bitter Personal Encounter
Perhaps the best way to begin telling the story of the uniqueness and novelty of Postcolonial Networks and Borderless Press is to tell the story of my first encounter with the politics of the world of publishing. In 2014, I was one happy man. I had worked through seven years of graduate school and produced a wonderful doctoral project. As soon as I was done I wanted to have it published. The

publication was imperative to me since it would boost my credentials for an academic job search. As we say in our business, "you publish or you perish." But more importantly I looked forward to have my ideas contribute to the understanding of the complexity of the questions of racial/ethnic conflicts and resolutions thereof. So I made contacts with a couple of publishing companies. I finally decided to go with Peter Lang for two reasons; their turnaround was only about six months, and I was acquainted with the editor of their imprint program, "Bible and Theology in Africa." However, in order to be published with Peter Lang I had to pay a subvention fee of $3,700, whch included typesetting fees. This was a huge setback. But I paid the money with the understanding that I would recoup it from the royalties.[129] To my surprise when the book was finally published, it was priced at $87. The price effectively put the book out of reach of my primary target audience or the general academic audience for that matter. I made several protest inquiries about the overprice, but I quickly found out that even if I had known prior to publication I would have had no say in the pricing process. Needless to say, I have come to accept the possibility that I will never recover the money I put into the publication.

The above practices are not unique to Peter Lang. Increasingly more and more publication presses operate more or less the same way. Those that do not charge subvention fees give negligible royalties. They also have strict standards for publication including language conventions that are outside the sociocultural and linguistic practices of most Majority World contexts. As a result, major publish-

---

[129]. Some authors are not asked upfront about subvention fees. But they are paid minimal royalties. Either way the author is always the loser while the publishing corporate machine takes all the profits of their labor.

ing companies, knowingly or unknowingly, participate in colonial epistemic knowledge practices. By charging subvention fees, they disadvantage Majority World scholars who cannot afford to pay such fees. And by pricing the books beyond the Majority World means of income (and the income of an average academic community) they, by implication, make books a reserve of Euro-American readership. Thus even a work written by a Majority World scholar becomes a property of the Euro-American publishing centers and their Euro-American readership. This center must have everything! I also realized during the production and sale of my book that once the publisher has made their cut (made their money off the book) they move on to the next catch. During the year when my book was published (2014), it was put up on a sale stand at the American Academy of Religion and the Society of Biblical Literature annual conference. The following year the book was not displayed. When I asked why, I was told that Peter Lang only puts the books on sale at the annual meeting once during the year that they are published. I learned the bitter truth that in the course of the year new books get published and the publisher must move on and make profit from the next "victim" of the system.

    The painful experience with my first publication has to do with the impersonal relationship between the major Euro-American publishers and the authors. These publication companies have no moral and ethical responsibility towards the author. Their interactions with the authors start at the point of acquiring the author's book project and ends with the publication of the book. Their purpose to get the project through their production machinery as quickly as possible in order to get their profit and move on to the next project. Their job and relationship with the author is strictly business oriented, rotating around a legal binding contract that disadvantages the author including taking away the author's rights to his/her own work while paying the author peanuts for it.

It is this system, among others, that Borderless Press seeks to change. Our relationship with the author begins long before their books are published and lasts long after their books are published.

Borderless Press: A Different Kind of Press

Borderless Press offers unique services to support the publication journey of our Majority World scholars.

SCHOLARLY WRITING AND PUBLISHING WORKSHOPS

At Borderless Press we proceed from the idea that encountering the "face" is the most fruitful starting point for publication of manuscripts from Majority World contexts. So our process begins by taking a journey to a Majority World location to meet with the scholars in their everyday contexts of scholarship praxes. We get to spend time with the scholars, listening to their scholarly stories, examine their manuscripts, and share with them our knowledge and expertise on the politics of publishing from start to finish. We also bring along published authors who share their experiences of the art of writing a book. We started this practice with our first scholarly writing and publishing workshop in collaboration with St. Paul's University in Limuru, Kenya, in the summer of 2015. We were able to host fifty recent PhD graduates, graduate students, and faculty from six local Kenyan universities. This was followed by another Writers' and Publishing workshop at the same university in August 2016. We plan to keep offering the Scholarly Writing and Publishing Workshop each year at St. Paul's University in Limuru, Kenya, and hopefully spread to other parts of Africa and the rest of the Majority World in the near future. The workshops offer free, intensive, five-day writing and publishing workshops covering the information below.

- Overview of publishing from start to finish
- Abstracts, research proposals, literature reviews, arguments and indexes
- Citation and bibliographic styles
- Translation challenges and solutions
- Process of taking a doctoral thesis to publication as a book
- Global distribution of books previously published locally
- Electronic bibliographies and citation practices
- Proprietary images
- Ethical guidelines for ethnographic interviews

The workshops provide an avenue where we encourage even the timidest of the scholars to gain the courage to not only to publish their work, but we show them how to do it, offering to walk them through until they get published. We hope that if we can continue holding these workshops we will generate a continuous and increasing number of publications from the Majority World scholars. If this happens, we will have joined the decolonizing bandwagon that will address the problem, earlier alluded to, in the work of Dabashi who asks, Can Non-Europeans Think? We will simply parade our many publications to answer that question.

Following the workshop, we work with authors to develop relationships whose goal is to get their work published. Authors also have the opportunity for additional coaching which includes pre-peer review (see below) and copy editing services.[130]

PRE-PEER REVIEW

Once the workshop is done, we exchange contacts and invite manuscripts (most often their unpublished doctoral projects). Thus, unlike Euro-American major publications, when we receive the manuscripts we receive them from "our friends." They know us and we know them. Once the manuscripts arrive at our desks we do what we call scan-reading (a quick read through) to determine the potential for publication. Once we are convinced that the work meets the standard for publication we identify a senior scholar in the area of specialty of the manuscript and ask them to do what we call pre-peer review process. The pre-peer review process is similar to the double-blind peer review process in terms of expectations of academic peer reviewed work. However, the difference is that the pre-peer review is not a double-blind process. The pre-peer reviewer and the scholar can know each other and sometimes interact in the process of exchanging ideas on the manuscript. The pre-peer reviewer prepares a detailed analysis of the project in terms of its strengths, weaknesses, articulation of the thesis statement, answering the research question(s), and meeting the standards of academic writing among other things. Once we receive these comments, we forward them to the author who begins revising their projects as per the comments. We pride ourselves as being pioneers in this area as far as publication houses are concerned. We have noticed

---

130. As we write this book, twelve scholars out of our 2015 and 2016 workshops at St. Paul's University have submitted their book projects to Borderless Press for publication. We are at various working stages with these scholars to have their books published.

in our work with Majority scholars, that unlike their Euro-American counterparts, Majority scholars do not have a system where friends can read their work and consistently offer feedback to make it better. Beyond the doctoral committees, these scholars have no scholarly support; hence many of the doctoral projects never get published. Our pre-peer review process fills this gap.

Most often Majority World book projects are rejected by Minority World publishers on the pretext that they do not meet publication standards. Our pre-peer review process is the first step in the decolonizing process of this Eurocentric mentality that measures Majority World scholars using Minority World epistemological knowledge systems. The process dismantles this myth by preparing high-quality book projects that meet not only meets Minority World standards, but ones that are cognizant of the Majority World epistemological nuances.

MENTOR-SCHOLAR SERVICES

Depending on the pre-peer review comments, our next stage in the process is to assign the Majority World scholars a mentor — a service that no any other publication company offers. Most often these are senior and experienced scholars in the academic area that the Majority World is working in. This senior scholar will work with the Majority World scholar chapter by chapter, almost in a similar manner of supervising a doctoral project. The senior scholar will help the Majority World scholar to work through all of the comments suggested by the pre-peer reviewer and any other issues that the senior scholar may notice in the project. The purpose of this process is to make sure that the final product meets all of the requirements to go through a successful double-blind peer review. The mentors do not impose their understanding on the work of the Majority World junior scholar. They rather act as guides to help the junior scholar articulate their own voices.

GLOBAL WRITING AND PUBLISHING FELLOWSHIPS

Once the senior scholar and the Majority World scholar have worked through the project, the senior scholar and the young Majority World scholar send a report to Postcolonial Networks/Borderless Press editor to the effect that the project is ready for double-blind peer review. The Borderless Press editor then identifies and solicits the services of a scholar to do double-blind peer review of the project. Once this is done and Borderless Press has received the comments from the reviewer, Postcolonial Networks/Borderless Press offers the final unique service which again no other publication company offers. We invite a scholar to the USA, Europe, or any other part of the world to get concentrated time and resources to write their final project as per the double-blind peer reviewer's analysis and comments. Often times we work with partners from the universities and private sector to create what we call a three-months writing residency. This writing residency offers the Majority World scholar a free paid air-ticket trip to the designated location, some stipend for personal effects, free room and board, an office space, a computer, and unlimited access to a modern library/books. The purpose of the residency is to allow a Majority World scholar concentrated time to finish writing their book project.

In return for the hospitality of the host institution, the Majority World scholar offers lectures to students and professors to the host institutions in relation to their research projects. The scholar and the host institutions can also build long-term relationships that may flow into future sabbatical research/teaching exchanges between the host institution and the home institution of the Majority World scholar. The decolonizing effect of this reciprocal relationship flows from the understanding that the Majority World scholar is a partner with the Minority World academy in the common efforts to produce knowledge for our common world.

At the end of the residency the scholar gives the finished manuscript to the Borderless Press editor who does the final checks and prepares the manuscript for publication.

BORDERLESS PUBLISHING POLICIES

Throughout all the above processes, Postcolonial Networks/ Borderless Press, through the financial support of donors, shoulders all the financial responsibilities. Whereas it costs money to organize the Writing and Publishing workshop we do not ask the invited Majority World scholars to pay for any of the costs. In our practices we also seek to minimize editorial and reviewer costs by asking experienced senior scholars to donate their time to do this free of charge. Similarly, whereas most publication companies charge the author subvention fees, especially if they determine the marketability of the book to be low, Borderless Press does not. We seek to publish our books at the cheapest prices possible and without any charge to the author regardless of the marketability value of the book.

PARTNERING WITH BORDERLESS PRESS

As you can see from the above Borderless Press cartography, we offer unique services that no any other publishing company does. We offer these services in the spirit of knowledge activism that seeks to change the status quo of Eurocentric knowledge epistemological framework. Our purpose is to see a continuous increase in the production, distribution, and consumption of work from Majority World scholars. We also seek to change the ethics/morals and values of the publishing industry. Most Euro-American major publishing companies are profit-making companies that make colossal amounts of money off of the authors. They do this by either making the authors pay for the costs of the books they publish or pricing the books at very high prices. The end result is that both the author and average reader do not benefit from the process. Here is how we seek to change this. We seek to reduce the cost of publication of books as much as possible so that we can price our books at reasonable and affordable prices.

But in order to be able to offer the above services, we seek to rely on another decolonizing premise which is that we all have a moral and ethical responsibility to support Majority World scholarship. This moral responsibility would require financial, property, and intellectual donations. We welcome financial donations to Postcolonial Networks/Borderless Press to continue hosting workshops and providing residencies to Majority World scholars. As we write this book all the people that work for us are volunteer workers. But to make this work effective and reach out to many Majority World scholars we look forward to having the money to enable us to hire some full-time staff. In terms of property help, we require universities and private individuals to work with us to host Majority World scholars for a period of three months at a time in order that these scholars can get concentrated time to finalize their manuscripts for publication. In terms of intellectual donation, we need scholars who would be willing to donate their time to do pre-peer review, provide mentorship and also do double-blind review. We also ask those university libraries, scholars, and all people of goodwill to purchase the Majority World books. Additionally, we look forward to a time when professors at teaching institutions would go beyond their biases and assign Majority World books to their classes and also cite the Majority World scholarship in their work. In doing all these we would become one family working for a better educated and informed world where no part of the world's scholarship is outside academic consumption. We dream for a world where knowledge from all geopolitical parts of our planet has a role to play in the common good of humanity — and where Majority World scholarship has a significant pie of that responsibility if given the chance in the sense that this body of scholarship flows from ethical questions of researching as demonstrated below.

C. *Knowledge Activism*: **Knowledge for Social Change** — Wafula

Research Question as a Reflection of Sociopolitical and Economic Mirror of the Researcher

Majority World scholarships often proceed and flow out of a deep reflection and wrestling with sociopolitical and economic questions of their geopolitical locations. There is so much at stake for us that disinterested abstract scholarship is a luxury. We witness senselessness all around us all the time: People dying from preventable diseases, poverty-stricken families with millions living in inhuman conditions, lack of food, lack of access to education, rampart corruption in governments, ethnic/tribal wars, poor road and housing infrastructure, among a host of other issues. We are products of a long history of colonization and neo-colonization to the extent that each successive generation of Majority World scholars realizes that they have to become a part of a long history of resistance to make the world a better place. Since Majority World life is a life in constant danger, we take seriously the wisdom contained in the words of Elie Wiesel that in times of crisis and of danger to a human life, no one has the right to choose caution, or abstention. We agree that when the life of so many is at stake, neutrality positions that allow some to do nothing to solve society's problems, is a criminal activity.[131] In light of this we take our lessons from Martin Luther King Jr. who stated: "It may well be that we will have to repent in this generation. Not merely for the vitriolic words and the violent actions of the bad people, but for the appalling silence and indifference of the good people who sit around and say, 'Wait on time.'"[132] Yes, for the Majority World scholars waiting on time while knowledge of whole continents goes to waste is a criminal act.

Thus in our contexts, we have a deep commitment to the issues that affect the common people. That is why our research is so important not just for us in the Majority World but can be an eye-opener for Euro-American contexts as well. It can help moderate the Western obsession with abstract scholarship and perhaps bridge the gap between the ivory tower academicians and the lives of common people in Euro-American contexts. Thus when I wrote my *Biblical Representations of Moab: A Kenyan Postcolonial Reading*, I chose to narrate the intricate relationships between the Israelites and the Moabites in the Hebrew Bible alongside the stories of the postcolonial Kikuyu and Luo people in Kenya to make a case that postcolonial narratives are the foundation upon which institutions are built. Institutions in turn

---

131. Elie Wiesel, *Messengers of God: Biblical Portraits and Legends* (New York: Summit Books, 1976), 213.

132. Martin Luther King, Jr., "Quotes," *A Testament of Hope: The Essential Writings and Speeches*, accessed January 26, 2016, http://www.goodreads.com/quotes/803418-it-may-well-be-that-we-will-have-to-repent.

enact practices which create either interethnic violence or peace, especially in multiracial/ethnic communities. In the process I make a case that for one to build a more peaceful and just multiracial/ethnic society, one needs to pay careful attention to how stories are told in order to encourage and nurture stories that create interracial/ethnic peace while at the same time deconstruct and hopefully dismantle stories that nurture violence.[133] I take up this burden in the context of interethnic hate speech, violence, and killings in Kenya. In doing this I follow the long tradition of Kenyan and African scholars that have taken up burdens ranging from ethnicity, religious violence, patriarchy, gender violence, political corruption, diseases (HIV/Aids, Ebola) and so forth.

At Postcolonial Networks and Borderless Press, we are aware that the same burden is in the hearts of many other Majority World scholars who wish to write their stories but have never had the opportunity to do so. In the summer of 2015, Postcolonial Networks organized a workshop at St. Paul's university in Limuru Kenya (as stated elsewhere in this book). During one of the sessions we asked all scholars present to talk about their academic journeys and why they wish to write. Scholar after scholar talked about what bothers them and the burdens they carry on their shoulders for their communities. We heard stories about child abuse, women violence, election rigging, tribalism, and the list went on and on. It is these scholars and their untold stories that we at Postcolonial Networks/Borderless Press are concerned about. We want their stories told. We want them to become a part of the academic narratives in the world.

---

133. Wafula, *Biblical Representations of Moab*, see particularly chapter 5.

VI. CHANGES THAT LIBERATE COLONIAL KNOWLEDGE

Joseph F. Duggan

The closed knowledge system is not likely to open unless we change the location of value in the publishing process. The universal value in both Majority World print shops and major academic presses is exactly the same. The highest priority is to recover costs and make a profit at the expense of authors and the availability of their high quality scholarship. Supply-and-demand economics will keep the intellectual knowledge system closed and ensure strenuous resistance to any *knowledge activist* actions that attempt to disrupt and open the system.

Every alternative technology including open-access publishing has inculturated us to ask the question: Who will pay for the production of the content? Scholars have fully bought into the corporate benefits of the military-industrial complex that their critical theories continue to reject. They reject the military corporate industrial economics in the comfort of their theoretical development, but they have not challenged their departments' tenure processes, university library purchasing decisions, reevaluated their own placement of value to be paid to write even — if in the minuscule royalties they still feel entitled to have. All at the same time they have not questioned who is not at the publishing table, due to their own privileged entitlements. *Knowledge activism* seeks to change this uninterrupted system of continued colonial dominance through a worldwide call to action.

Through almost a decade of Postcolonial Networks' work with Majority World authors we have learned firsthand about the crippling impact of the dominant knowledge production system and publishing economics. Many Majority World authors have attained their doctorates from major North American, European and South African universities in addition to a number of smaller, less known Majority World universities. Most scholars who return after their doctorate to their home nation face many of the same obstacles as North Americans and Europeans to publishing their first book. However, many authors return to a culture where they have more family responsibilities due to the prevalence of multi-generational extended families, live in villages with limited or nonexistent Wi-Fi services and lack continuous access to the latest scholarship in their chosen discipline. Unless scholars publish their book immediately their scholarship quickly becomes stale and they face even more severe impediments to publishing with a publisher that is able to get their work out to readers around the world albeit in major research libraries and out of reach of their Majority World students due to exorbitant costs.

Slow Change
Postcolonial Networks and Borderless Press have exited the corporatized system of production that has served the few at the expense of many, especially Majority World scholars and other authors in this context. It is likely to take a complete shutdown of the academic publishing

closed-knowledge system before many academic independent presses are able to function as for-profit publishers. If tenure continues to be offered in fewer and fewer higher education institutions, eventually scholar-authors will have little incentive to choose to publish their book with a prestigious academic publisher. Increasingly a new generation of scholars want their books broadly accessible to as many different constituencies as possible. Eventually I predict the power will shift from the places of higher education and the publishing houses to the authors and readers. The entire academic closed-knowledge system will experience the equivalence of economic deregulation.

Some scholars around the world are already publishing their own books through access to free self-publishing software. While given all the publishing challenges already stated above and the desire to communicate one's work, self-publishing makes total sense. Unfortunately, all too many scholars use self-publishing without fully understanding the scholarly publishing process. I have read a number of self-published academic books and these volumes often substantially fall short in areas of copyediting, citations and even arguments. It is thoroughly understandable that with a closed knowledge system that these self-publishing actions would be perceived as knowledge activist interventions. Although self-publishing appears to be the most disruptive knowledge activist intervention, it is not, because poorly crafted books just further marginalize Majority World scholars.

Disruptive Publishing
Postcolonial Networks as a nonprofit has not established Borderless Press to make a profit. Borderless Press was exclusively established to ally with Majority World scholars in ways that imitate the closed knowledge system's

network of support. We share these patterns of support through our pre-peer reviewers, scholar mentors and writing residencies. Borderless Press is now a completely voluntary organization. We have no cost to publish a book because an increasing number of *knowledge activists* have joined our coalition as professional volunteers to disrupt the closed knowledge system and open up new contributions to scholarship.

Waiting for the closed knowledge system to purchase our books was a time-consuming exercise that required enormous patience and innocent trust that the corporate-industrial complex would heal itself of its own institutional racism and exclusion of Majority World authors. We could invest in developing institutional relationships with major research libraries so that they would purchase our books on a rotating cycle as they purchase the major academic publishers' books. The sale of our books at reduced costs consistently provokes the capitalist knowledge broker to continue to diminish the value of the Majority World author's contribution. If the book is cheap to purchase it must have no value.

As discussed in the last chapter the entire life cycle of the book begins and ends with the author's social relation. Most often the research question originates with the author's familial, tribal or village experience. Authors tend to ask research questions that they hope eventually will bring wholeness to their family, tribe or village as the beginning of scholar activism that will impact an entire discipline and even a nation and one day the world. These are bold research questions that are not about empty, sterile arguments that lack personal stories. The best books are inspired out of a hunger and thirst for justice in the author's own communities.

The creation of the book on these sacred terms must also change the way the book is distributed to potential readers. Majority World authors understand the process of brokering their knowledge to those who need it. Many Majority World authors are not motivated by tenure process as many African universities lack such a process of entitlement. Most Majority World scholars have no preconceived notions about fame or royalties from their book. Of course Majority World authors would like to be treated fairly, but like the vast majority of all scholar-authors they lack familiarity with the internal processes of capitalist, profit-centered publishers.

To disrupt the dominant distribution patterns that are dependent on consumers to value Majority World scholarship, *knowledge activists* must take a different path forward. Postcolonial Networks and Borderless Press sees the book as an invitation to be in a relationship and scholarly conversation. We send our books to faculty who might include one of our books in their syllabi, and we selectively offer our books to libraries where we have supporters of our work. Increasingly we will seek to locate our books where research is being done and our authors are most likely to be cited. Of course we continue to sell our books and seek financial sustainability, but our *knowledge activist* decisions are not based on sales or profits as are academic publishers. We are not alone in this regard. Many small academic presses are managed and led by voluntary scholars who do the work with incredible passion for quality scholarship and not for profit. We have extended this passion as a means to decolonize knowledge production and distribution.

Through our writing and publishing residencies we seek to foster and facilitate new scholarly friendships for our Majority World authors that yield new collaborations that lead to new research opportunities, meetings and co-authored works. We hope that by changing the publishing ecosystem through relationships and friendships, we imitate the relationships formed in the closed knowledge system but in a way that does not seek to temporarily open and then quickly close again, rather for scholars to see a means to learn from Majority World authors how their work may become more responsive to oppression, beyond theory into praxis. We envision international collaborations that reciprocally learn from one another.

At the outset of this chapter I told the story of the weekly Facebook posts by scholars and the disdain of a few for overly priced scholarly books that oppressed communities and many others cannot afford to purchase. From this chapter I hope readers see that it is not all about the book's price, but it is about a closed knowledge system and its privileged economics that oppresses many for the benefit of a few. Major academic publishers justifiably deserve critique, but these critiques must not exclusively be lodged on publishers alone. Scholar-authors and readers must become informed about the closed knowledge system in which they participate. The beneficiaries of the closed knowledge system, acting together as *knowledge activists*, have the opportunity to disrupt the closed knowledge system in ways that all voices are heard, or they can continue to be silent and occasionally register their bourgeoisie complaint but make no effort to demand change.

Postcolonial Networks and Borderless Press are not alone in our *knowledge activism. Knowledge activism* as two words brought together is new, but there are many other *knowledge activists* working in other areas too. Readers will have the opportunity to hear from two of these *knowledge activists* in the final part of this book. We could fill an entire volume with stories of other *knowledge activists*. Beyond the two *knowledge activists* in the final part of this book are many more activists working behind the scenes to influence and disrupt other parts of the closed knowledge system. All *knowledge activists* do vital work to the future decolonize knowledge systems, but most are rendered invisible by the corporate machine.

Global knowledge poverty will be alleviated as we change our values to align with the world's knowledge hunger. Like most profitable machines most of these changes will not come by choice but rather through a complete disruption of the higher education and publishing status quo. In the existing system marginalization of Majority World scholars contributes to the scarcity of knowledge and perpetuates supply-demand economics. In the meantime, concentrated efforts will demonstrate some openings but the entire system remains closed until *knowledge activism* becomes widespread.

Conclusions — Wafula and Duggan

In this book we have just scratched the surface of that which is needed to decolonize knowledge systems and allow Majority World scholars a place in the world's production of knowledge. We started by laying out the contours of contemporary epistemological imbalances in the world between Majority World and Minority World where Minority World is the major player in the production, distribution, and consumption of knowledge. We have demonstrated the various hegemonic controls that make this dominance possible. We show how we can all work together to balance out the production, distribution, and consumption of knowledge. We ask that each one of us take our social and ethical responsibility towards helping the marginalized Majority World publish more. We not only theorize how this can be done but through Borderless Press demonstrate the praxis that we are doing to address the problem. We hope that our contribution is the first in Borderless Press' series of *knowledge activism* books. If you have been energized by this book, but felt we should have addressed or further developed another area, we invite you to consider writing a book for our *knowledge activism* series or offer a critical review of our book to encourage us to write a second one. We welcome contributions in fields such as library science, linguistics, languages, and translation, among others. We welcome books that particularly address issues and methodologies of specific Majority World contexts. We also welcome books on the decolonization of the universities.

APPENDIX:
KNOWLEDGE ACTIVISM SELF-ASSESSMENT AND DEVELOPMENT

In order to help readers move from this book and further develop their *knowledge activism* awareness and praxis responding to our worldwide call to action, we have developed the following preliminary questions as a self-assessment and development tool. We fully admit the first generation nature of this tool. We hope our proposed tool will be the cause of additional conversation and in future books lead to the further development of this tool and the development of additional tools that promote *knowledge activism*. Our questions are by no means comprehensive. We hope readers will build upon these initial questions as together we foster and expand a *knowledge activism* movement. In each category below we have listed ten questions in hopes to provoke and inspire additional questions. Our desire is to initiate a conversation that begins to enhance awareness and ask questions that have not often been asked before. Every actor in the knowledge system has a responsibility for the choices they make and the blind eye they turn that would otherwise promote decolonial literature.

The first two questions for all of us are what is our ethical responsibility as a *knowledge activist* and what sacrifices are we willing to make so that every author has the opportunity to publish their book, to be read and also to be cited by other scholars?

In answering these two questions in the affirmative we begin to accept responsibility for our shared colonial history as one that has allowed some authors to remain silent in the academy to the detriment of all knowledge.

Authors

- Are my needs as an author the only needs that matter when I choose a publisher, or am I responsible to work with publishers who have a commitment to justice and anti-oppression beyond mere content?
- What is my ethical responsibility as an author to choose a publisher whose organization's practice models *knowledge activism*?
- Is it an ethical problem that compromises my book's justice and anti-oppression argument when I purchase a book from a publisher whose business model does not support my principles and authors from marginalized communities, nations and universities?
- Have I made an effort to include works from Majority World nations?
- Does my bibliography include sources from scholars around the world, especially the Majority World?
- In my citations have I effectively narrated the contributions of all authors, especially from marginalized communities and nations?
- Am I concerned about the price of the book and the limits it will place on widespread access to the book?

- Am I concerned that my publisher has no economically feasible distribution channels in the Majority World in Africa, Asia and South America?
- Have I selected a publisher that helps me match my argument to my praxis?
- Do my publisher's editorial boards include fair representation of scholars from Majority World universities and nations?

Readers

- Is it an ethical problem that compromises my justice and anti-oppression commitments when I purchase a book from a publisher whose business model does not support authors from marginalized communities, nations and universities?
- What effort do I make to understand the ethical principles of the publishers of the books I read and cite in my work?
- Do my decisions to purchase from certain publishers compromise my justice and anti-oppression commitments?
- What responsibility do I have as a reader to purchase books from publishers who treat the authors of my books with dignity and respect?
- How many of my books in my personal library are published by independent presses?
- How many of the books in my personal library are published by authors from marginalized communities and nations?
- What is my writing standard of scholarship?
- Do I expect to read perfect American or British English as the standard of good academic scholarship?
- What space do I make for indigenous authors and indigenous methodologies?

- How seriously do I take books that have no citations or sources from authors in Majority World nations?

Researchers and Doctoral Candidates

- Who authorizes me to think, write, speak and is it my innate right to do so, or do I believe my doctoral committee and those who award me my degree give me the privilege to think, write, speak and contribute?
- What risks am I willing to take as I ask my research question, choose my methodology and develop my argument?
- What is my ethical responsibility to connect my argument to my praxis, justice and anti-oppression principles?
- Will my research question make an urgent difference to a socio-political need of a real community that suffers?
- Am I passionately committed to my research question or is it just a question to demonstrate my adeptness as a scholar?
- Do I know the authors and scholars working in my discipline and research area around the world especially in Africa, Asia and South America or do I only know and read scholars in North America and Europe?
- Have I been in conversation with scholars around the world, and have I made an effort to diversify my data collection sources beyond privileged portals?
- What do my footnotes and bibliography tell me about the scope of my knowledge that I privilege as contributors to my argument?
- Does my doctoral committee reflect the complexity of the discipline and research area, or have I prioritized one set of privileged ideas to the exclusion of others, especially outside my geographical location?

- Do I see any gaps in my research process that go against my justice and anti-oppression principles so that I make different choices upon completion of my PhD, or will I continue to comply with the knowledge system that rewards me with tenure and other rewards?

Masters and Doctoral Supervisors

- Have I held my masters and doctoral candidates responsible for the breadth of the scholarly literature in their discipline even when it is a challenge to access?
- Have I ever rendered a master's thesis or doctoral dissertation incomplete due to an absence of any citations from authors and scholars in Africa, Asia and South America?
- Have I challenged my students' scholarly integrity to match their research question, methodology, argument and contribution to the needs of all people, or do I detect privilege in their argument?
- What have I told my students about the relationship between ethics and research and how do these principles change the academy through my work and that of my students' research?
- Do the bibliographies I distribute for comprehensive exams include scholarship from scholars working in the Majority World?
- Do I discount the *knowledge activism* concerns of my students and promote compliance versus speaking up to make change through their thinking?
- What are my needs as a supervisor for affirmation and even intellectual submission by my students?
- Have I made an effort to advocate for Majority World researchers in my department?
- Have I initiated collaborations with Majority World scholars to model to my students the ways we must change the knowledge system?

- Do my books reflect the breadth of knowledge that I expect from my students, especially in the ways I cite literature from Africa, Asia and South America?

Copy Editors

- What is my ethical responsibility as a copy editor to authors, publishers and readers?
- What effort have I made to understand the author's voice in context before I seek to standardize the manuscript to my preferred, privileged, universal set of principles?
- What are the power relations between copy editor, author and publisher?
- What is my tone of questions to authors, and do I shame authors whose first language is not English?
- If the author's argument is coherent, do I seek to align the manuscript to a universal standard of English sanitizing local voice?
- What does it mean for me to maintain the author's voice?
- Does my editing style dominate and sanitize the author's voice and cultural context?
- What copy editing practices do I need to change in order not to sanitize an author's voice and culture?
- Is the form of my copy editing suggestions such as track changes important or are some forms inherently colonial?
- As a professional copy editor, what concerns do I have about my professional practice and the ways I unintentionally marginalize authors whose first language is not English?

University Librarians

- What is my ethical responsibility to students and faculty in purchase decisions and the library's budget allocated to Majority World scholarship?

- Have I exercised influence across the university as I collaborate with faculty on the development of their bibliographies and syllabi to make sure that scholars and authors around the world are included in our resources?
- What effort have I made to introduce Majority World scholarship to faculty and students when they seek quality research?
- What responsibility do I accept to assess the privileged characteristics of the library's research tools and what effort have I made to correct deficiencies?
- Am I sufficiently aware of the Majority World composition of the library's resources, including books?
- Have I made an effort to be knowledgeable in indigenous methodologies and other research resources not common in North America and Europe?
- Am I aware of my research biases and the impact on the books we purchase in our university's library?
- Am I aware of the faculty's research biases and the impact on the books our library provides to our students?
- Am I willing to be an active influencer who demonstrates to faculty the need to diversify resources?
- Have I made an effort to promote *knowledge activism* changes to the university's administration or through my purchasing power with the major publishers who provide our library's books?

Peer Reviewers

- Am I familiar with all the literature of my discipline and the author's research area, especially in the Majority World?
- Have I informed publishers that my knowledge of the discipline is limited to North America and Europe when I am unaware of the scholarly contributions of Majority World scholars?

- Would I ever disqualify myself as a peer reviewer to the publisher when my knowledge of the discipline has been limited to North America and Europe, and I am unaware of the scholarly contributions of Majority World scholars?
- Have I asked authors for some evidence of their research efforts when there are no Majority World scholarly works in their bibliography related to their research question and argument?
- Am I concerned about the scholarly integrity of the scholarship I am reviewing due to the absence of contributions from one significant part of the world?
- How do I treat authors whose first language is not English?
- What are my reading principles and in what ways do they disadvantage the manuscripts of authors whose first language is not English?
- How as a peer reviewer can I more effectively decolonize knowledge?
- Should peer reviewers be compensated for their service and does their fee in any way compromise the rigorous independence of the scholarly process?
- How will these questions change the way I write and produce knowledge as a scholar and when I work with students in the classroom or as a doctoral supervisor?

Department Heads and University Presidents

- How effective are we in the promotion of Majority World scholarship when we evaluate tenure applications and approve doctoral projects?
- How effective are my faculty in their promotion of knowledge and research from around the world especially from Africa, Asia and South America in their syllabi, bibliographies and other teaching documents?

- How do we financially support Majority World scholarship?
- How often do we invite scholars from the Majority World to our research collaborations?
- How do we use our power and privilege to change academic disciplines?
- How do we use our power and privilege to influence publishers and the choices they make?
- How does our university press model *knowledge activism*?
- How do we advocate for Majority World scholars?
- How are we working with other research universities so that through our collective power we decolonize knowledge?
- What have the costs been to knowledge production for the ways we have been historically silent and complacent in failing to challenge colonial knowledge and postpone decolonial knowledge?

Academic Publishers

- What is my ethical responsibility to academic readers and research university librarians to provide Majority World scholarship?
- How does our organization's publishing philosophy promote or impede the integrity of knowledge through the full inclusion of authors from all over the world, especially in Majority World contexts?
- How does our pricing philosophy impact all libraries' access to knowledge?
- What has been our commitment to innovative distribution channels for economically deprived nations and universities?
- How vigilant have we been in inviting Majority World scholars to serve on editorial boards?

- How effective have we been in appointing Majority World chairs of editorial boards where the content is Majority World in its sourcing?
- Do we have a policy that privileges the selection of double-blind peer reviewers from only North America or Europe?
- Have we made it a priority to select double-blind peer reviewers who will fairly read manuscripts whose author's first language is not English?
- Do we have ethical principles that help us determine just profits, compensation of editors and author royalties?
- What efforts have we made to publish books in languages other than English?

BIBLIOGRAPHY

Achebe, Chinua. *Home and Exile*. New York, NY: Anchor Books, 2000.

Ajani, Timothy T. "Is There Indeed A "Nigerian English?" *Journal of Humanities & Social Sciences* 1, No. 1 (2007): No Pages. Accessed April 1, 2016. http://www.scientificjournals.org/journals2007/articles/1084.htm.

Anzaldúa, Gloria. *Borderlands/La Frontera: The New Mestiza*. Aunt Lute, San Francisco, 1987.

Benyawa, Linah. "Public Universities Promoting Tribalism in Kenya, NCIC Warns." Standard, August 8, 2015. No pages. Accessed 20 January 2016. http://www.standardmedia.co.ke/article/2000172071/public- universities-promoting-tribalism-in-kenya-ncic-warns.

Breier, Mignonne. "Africa: How Africa Is Tackling 'Next Generation Fears in Academia." No Pages. Accessed November 2, 2015. http://allafrica.com/stories/201510301485.html?aa_source=nwsltr-education-en.

Carvalhaes, Cláudio. *Liturgy in Postcolonial Perspectives: Only One is Holy*. New York: Palgrave, 2015.

Cone, James Hal. *Black Theology and Black Power*. Maryknoll, NY: Orbis Books, 1967.

Dabashi, Hamid. *Can Non-Europeans Think?* London: Zed Books, 2015.

DeGruy, Joy. *Post Traumatic Slave Syndrome: America's Legacy of Enduring Injury and Healing*. Portland, OR: Joy DeGruy Publications, Inc., 2005.

Dei, George J. Sefa. *Teaching Africa: Towards a Transgressive Pedagogy*. New York, NY: Springer Publishers, 2012.

Freire, Paulo. *Pedagogy of the Oppressed*, 30th edition. London; New York, NY: Continuum, 2000.

Grande, Sandy. *Red Pedagogy: Native American Social and Political Thought*. Lanham, MD: Rowman & Littlefield Publishers, 2004.

Grosfoguel, Ramón. ""Decolonizing Post-Colonial Studies and Paradigms of Political Economy: Transmodernity, Decolonial Thinking, and Global Coloniality." Transmodernity: Journal of Peripheral Cultural Production of the Luso-Hispanic World 1 No. 1 (2011): No pages. Accessed April 2, 2016. http://dialogoglobal.com/texts/grosfoguel/Grosfoguel-Decolonizing-Pol-Econ-and-Postcolonial.pdf.

Heaney, Robert S. *From Historical to Critical Post-Colonial Theology: The Contribution of John S. Mbiti and Jesse N. K. Mugambi*. Eugene: Pickwick Publications, 2016.

Jagessar Michael N., and Stephen Burns. *Christian Worship: Postcolonial Perspectives*. London: Routledge, 2011.

Karin, Jennifer Harvey. Case and Robin Hawley Gorsline, eds. *Dismantling White Supremacy From Within: White People On What We Need To Do*. Cleveland: The Pilgrim Press, 2008.

Kigotho, Wachira. "Are African Universities Ready for Diaspora Academics?" *University World News*. April 2, 2016. No pages. Accessed April 4, 2016. http://www.universityworldnews.com/article.php?story=20160401171348654.

King, Jr., Martin Luther. "Quotes." A Testament of Hope: The Essential Writings and Speeches, No pages. Accessed January 26, 016. Online: http://www.goodreads.com/quotes/803418-it-may-well-be-that-we-will-have-to-repent.

Levinas, Emmanuel. *Totality and Infinity: An Essay on Exteriority*. Translated by Alphonso Lingis. Pittsburgh, PA: Duquesne University Press, 1969.

Masenya (Ngwan'a Mphahlele), Madipoane. "For Ever trapped? An African Voice on Insider/Outsider Dynamics Within South African Old Testament Gender-Sensitive Frameworks." *The Old Testament Society of Southern Africa* 27 No. 1 (2014): 189–204.

Mbataru, Patrick. "Kenyan Universities Have Lost the Edge." Standard. September 20, 2016. Accessed September 20, 2016. http://www.standardmedia.co.ke/article/2000216751/kenyan-universities-have-lost-the-edge

Mbembe, Achille. *On the Postcolony*. Berkeley, CA: University of California Press, 2001.

McCarron, Richard E. "Kingdom Play? Striving Against Racisms through Worship in a Postcolonial Mode." *Liturgy* 29, No. 3 (2014): 47–54.

Memmi, Albert. *The Colonizer and the Colonized*. Boston, MA: Beacon Press, 1991.

Mignolo, Walter D. *Local Histories/Global Designs: Coloniality, Subaltern Knowledges, and Border Thinking*. Princeton, NJ: Princeton University Press, 2000.

_____. *The Dark Side of Western Modernity: Global Futures, Decolonial Options*. Durham, NC: Duke University Press, 2011.

Mudimbe, V.Y. *The Idea of Africa*. Bloomington and Indianapolis, IN: Indiana University Press, 1994.

_____. *The Invention of Africa: Gnosis, Philosophy, and the Order of Knowledge*. London: James Currey, 1988.

Narokobi, A. N. Emmanuel. "'Majority World' — A New Word for a New Age." No pages. *The Masalai Blog*. No pages. February 11, 2009. Accessed October 6 2016. https://masalai.wordpress.com/2009/02/11/majority-world-a-new-word-for-a-new-age/).

Ngabonziza, Dan and Jean de la Croix Tabaro. "Prof Romain Murenzi Reveals Africa's Academic Weakness." No Pages. Accessed 21 October 2015. Online: http://ktpress.rw/prof-romain-murenzi-reveals-africas-academic-weakness-3442.

Onstad, Eric. "WWII Lives on Among African Veterans Who Returned Home as Freedom Fighters." *Los Angeles Times*. November 5, 1989. No pages. Accessed April 1, 2016. http://articles.latimes.com/1989-11-05/news/mn-1369_1_world-war-ii.

Opiyo, Peter. "Shock of Tribalism in Public Universities." *Standard*. March 7, 2012. No pages. Cited 20 January 2016. http://www.standardmedia.co.ke/business/article/2000053553/shock-of-tribalism-in-public-universities.

Owino, Peres. "Bound: Africans Vs. African Americans. Peres Owino, "Bound: Africans vs. African Americans," Nyarnam Productions, 2014. Accessed January 18, 2016. https://itunes.apple.com/us/movie/bound-africans-vs-african/id989662587.

Pui-Lan, Kwok. *Postcolonial Imagination and Feminist Theology*. Westminster John Knox Press, Louisville, 2005.

Pui-lan, Kwok and Stephen Burns. *Postcolonial Practice of Ministry: Leadership, Liturgy, and Interfaith Engagement*. Lexington Books, Lanham, 2016.

Ricoeur, Paul. *Oneself as Another*. Translated by Kathleen Blamey. Chicago, IL: The University of Chicago Press, 1992.

Said, Edward W. *Orientalism*. New York, NY: Vintage Books, 1978.

Shah, Neha. "How Britain's Old Empire Lives on in Universities." *Guardian*. September 6. 2016. No pages. Accessed October 4, 2016. https://www.theguardian.com/education/2016/sep/06/how-britains-old-empire-lives-on-in-universities.

Smith, Lind Tuhiwai. *Decolonizing Methodologies: Research and Indigenous Peoples*, 2nd ed. London & New York, NY: Otago University Press, 2012.

Smith, James K. A. *Desiring the Kingdom, Worship, Worldview, and Cultural Formation*. Baker Academic, Grand Rapids, 2009.

Song, Angeline M.G. *A Postcolonial Woman's Encounter with Moses and Miriam*. New York, NY: Palgrave Macmillan, 2015.

Tossounian, Cecilia. "Review of Walter Mignolo." Bulletin of Latin American Research. *Journal of the Society for Latin American Studies* 33 No. 3 (2014): 370–372.

Wa Thiong'o, Ngũgĩ. *Decolonizing the Mind: The Politics of Language in African Literature*. Oxford and Nairobi: James Currey and Heinemann, 1986.

Wa Wamwere, Koigi. *Negative Ethnicity: From Bias to Genocide*. New York, NY: Seven Stories Press, 2003.

Wafula R.S. Wafula, *Biblical Representations of Moab: A Kenyan Postcolonial Reading*. New York, NY: Peter Lang, 2014.

_____. "What is Contextual hermeneutics? Justin S. Ukpong and Beyond." Pages 93–107 in *The Postcolonial Church: Theology, Identity, and Mission*. Edited by R.S. Wafula, Esther Mombo, and Joseph Wandera. Alameda, CA: Borderless Press, 2016.

West, Gerald. "Doing Postcolonial Biblical Interpretation @ Home: Ten of (South) African Ambivalence." *Neotestamentica* 42, no. 1 (2008): 147–164.

Wiesel, Elie. *Messengers of God: Biblical Portraits and Legends*. New York: Summit Books, 1976.

Zeleza, Paul Tiyambe. "Engagements Between African Diaspora Academics in the U.S. and Canada and African Institutions of Higher Education: Perspectives from North America and Africa." (November 2008): 1–37. Accessed 30 March 2016. http://www.iie.org/~/media/Files/Programs/Carnegie-African-Diaspora-Fellows-Program/Carnegie-Engage.

Other Websites Consulted

Vision. Carnegie African Diaspora Fellowship Program. No pages. Accessed April 5, 2016. http://www.iie.org/en/Programs/Carnegie-African-Diaspora-Fellows-Program/Vision.

Africa News Agency. "The Extent of Africa's Brain Drain is 'Frightening': Mbeki." August 15, 2015. No pages. Accessed January 20, 2016, https://www.enca.com/africa/extent-africa%E2%80%99s-brain-drain-frightening-mbeki.

"Tongues under Threat: English is Dangerously Dominant." *The Economist*. January 20, 2011. Accessed September 10 2016. http://www.economist.com/node/17963285.

Website of the British Library. "Magna Carta for the digital age 2015." *My Digital Rights Project*. June 15, 2015. No pages. Accessed September 10 2016. http://www.bl.uk/my-digital-rights/magna-carta-2015.

Academics Anonymous. "Academics are being hoodwinked into writing books nobody can buy." Guardian. September 4, 2015. Accessed September 10 2016. https://www.theguardian.com/higher-education-network/2015/sep/04/academics-are-being-hoodwinked-into-writing-books-nobody-can-buy.